Distributed Computing Pearls

Synthesis Lectures on Distributed Computing Theory

Editor

Michel Raynal, *University of Rennes, France and Hong Kong Polytechnic University*

Synthesis Lectures on Distributed Computing Theory is edited by Michel Raynal of the University of Rennes, France and Nancy Lynch of the Massachusetts Institute of Technology. The series publishes 50- to 150-page publications on topics pertaining to distributed computing theory. The scope largely follows the purview of premier information and computer science conferences, such as ACM PODC, DISC, SPAA, OPODIS, CONCUR, DialM-POMC, ICDCS, SODA, Sirocco, SSS, and related conferences. Potential topics include, but not are limited to: distributed algorithms and lower bounds, algorithm design methods, formal modeling and verification of distributed algorithms, and concurrent data structures.

Distributed Computing Pearls
Gadi Taubenfeld
2018

Decidability of Parameterized Verification
Roderick Bloem, Swen Jacobs, Ayrat Khalimov, Igor Konnov, Sasha Rubin, Helmut Veith, and Josef Widder
2015

Impossibility Results for Distributed Computing
Hagit Attiya and Faith Ellen
2014

Distributed Graph Coloring: Fundamentals and Recent Developments
Leonid Barenboim and Michael Elkin
2013

Distributed Computing by Oblivious Mobile Robots
Paola Flocchini, Giuseppe Prencipe, and Nicola Santoro
2012

Quorum Systems: With Applications to Storage and Consensus
Marko Vukolić
2012

Link Reversal Algorithms
Jennifer L. Welch and Jennifer E. Walter
2011

Cooperative Task-Oriented Computing: Algorithms and Complexity
Chryssis Georgiou and Alexander A. Shvartsman
2011

New Models for Population Protocols
Othon Michail, Ioannis Chatzigiannakis, and Paul G. Spirakis
2011

The Theory of Timed I/O Automata, Second Edition
Dilsun K. Kaynar, Nancy Lynch, Roberto Segala, and Frits Vaandrager
2010

Principles of Transactional Memory
Rachid Guerraoui and Michał Kapałka
2010

Fault-tolerant Agreement in Synchronous Message-passing Systems
Michel Raynal
2010

Communication and Agreement Abstractions for Fault-Tolerant Asynchronous
Distributed Systems
Michel Raynal
2010

The Mobile Agent Rendezvous Problem in the Ring
Evangelos Kranakis, Danny Krizanc, and Euripides Markou
2010

Distributed Computing Pearls
Gadi Taubenfeld

ISBN: 978-3-031-00884-9   paperback
ISBN: 978-3-031-02012-4   eBook
ISBN: 978-3-031-00130-7   hardcover

DOI 10.1007/978-3-031-02012-4

A Publication in the Springer series
SYNTHESIS LECTURES ON DISTRIBUTED COMPUTING THEORY

Lecture #14
Series Editor: Michel Raynal, *University of Rennes, France and Hong Kong Polytechnic University*
Founding Editor: Nancy Lynch, *Massachusetts Institute of Technology*
Series ISSN
Print 2155-1626   Electronic 2155-1634

Distributed Computing Pearls

Gadi Taubenfeld
The Interdisciplinary Center, Herzliya

SYNTHESIS LECTURES ON DISTRIBUTED COMPUTING THEORY #14

ABSTRACT

Computers and computer networks are one of the most incredible inventions of the 20th century, having an ever-expanding role in our daily lives by enabling complex human activities in areas such as entertainment, education, and commerce. One of the most challenging problems in computer science for the 21st century is to improve the design of distributed systems where computing devices have to work together as a team to achieve common goals.

In this book, I have tried to gently introduce the general reader to some of the most fundamental issues and classical results of computer science underlying the design of algorithms for distributed systems, so that the reader can get a feel of the nature of this exciting and fascinating field called distributed computing. The book will appeal to the educated layperson and requires no computer-related background. I strongly suspect that also most computer-knowledgeable readers will be able to learn something new.

KEYWORDS

algorithms, distributed algorithms, synchronization, agreement, consensus, synchronous, asynchronous, randomized algorithms, Byzantine agreement, choice coordination, the see-saw puzzle, the two lovers problem, the two generals problem, the too much bread problem, deadlock, dining philosophers, mutual exclusion, barrier synchronization, crash failures, Byzantine failures

To Miki,
the love of my life.

Contents

Preface

The design of distributed systems where computing devices (like computers, smartphones, sensors) interact with one another is one of the most challenging problems in computer science. In this book, I have tried to gently introduce the general reader to some of the most fundamental issues and classical results of computer science underlying the design of algorithms for distributed systems, so that the reader can get a feel of the nature of this exciting and interesting field. The book will appeal to the educated layperson and requires no computer-related background at all. I strongly suspect that also most computer-knowledgeable readers will be able to learn something new.

While humans can see and hear each other, computing devices usually communicate by sending messages or reading from and writing to shared memory locations. As a result, it is far more difficult to synchronize interactions between computers than between humans. Based on this observation, fundamental principles that relate to interactions between computing devices that involve concurrency and synchronization are explained throughout the book.

Each chapter deals with a specific topic presented in terms of a story. I have compared the issues that arise when dealing with groups of computing devices to those that arise when a group of people has to share their resources and work as a team in order to solve various problems together. Most chapters can be read in isolation, but there is a logical grouping to the complete set of chapters. The topics covered are not an exhaustive survey of the field of distributed computing, but largely a subjective sampling of its highlights.

One hint about reading this book—do not go too fast, try to read at most one chapter per sitting. Most of the problems presented look deceptively simple at first glance. The only way to understand their tricky nature is by trying to solve them yourself. For that reason, I suggest that, as soon as a problem is posted, you stop reading and try to solve it yourself. Only after you have butted your head against a problem for some time, can you appreciate its beauty. I hope you will enjoy reading the book!

Contact Information: Please feel free to contact me with any criticism or comments which you might have. I would be glad to hear from you! I can be reached by email at `tgadi@idc.ac.il` or by sending hardcopy mail to Prof. Gadi Taubenfeld, The Interdisciplinary Center, P.O.Box 167, Herzliya 46150, Israel.

Gadi Taubenfeld
May 2018

Acknowledgments

I would like to thank many of my colleagues for the influence they had on my work and therefore on this book. I thank Jennifer L. Welch and Michel Raynal for their helpful comments on a draft of the book. Most importantly, I thank my family for their love and support.

Gadi Taubenfeld
May 2018

CHAPTER 1

Distributed Computing

Two major developments that have happened in recent years are dramatically and irrevocably changing the computer landscape: the dramatic expansion in the use of the Internet, and the design of multicore computers where a single computer has multiple processors. A processor is the "brain" of the computer, and modern computers are now built with multiple "brains." In each one of these cases, processors on the same or different computers have to work together as a team to achieve common goals.

In addition to personal computers, smartphones, laptops, tablets, and webcams, the Internet offers connectivity between many other computing devices. A few examples are sensors which enable environmental monitoring applications; sensors which are used for monitoring changes in structural conditions of infrastructures like bridges; wearable sensors that can remotely read a patient's biometrics and send them to the patient's physician; infant monitors that provide parents with real-time information about their babies; and much more.

1.1 WINDS OF CHANGE

Computers and computer networks are one of the most incredible inventions of the 20th century, having an ever-expanding role in our daily lives by enabling complex human activities in areas such as entertainment, education, and commerce. One of the most challenging problems in computer science for the 21st century is to improve the design of systems where communicating devices interact with one another, and in particular, to invent new applications that will take advantage of these new capacities.

The fundamental changes in computing architectures, where the whole hardware industry shifted to both mobile and multicore platforms expanding the arena of communicating devices to an unprecedented scale, require a fundamental change in how applications are written for computer networks and multicore computers. Concurrency and synchronization are fundamental issues that are critical for the design of such applications—the Internet could not work without synchronized protocols, database systems would be unthinkable without them, operating systems would crash even more frequently, and concurrent programming would be an impossibility.

Concurrency exists, of course, not only in computer systems but also in nature and living organisms. We can find concurrency at the molecular level as well as at those of cells, organs, individuals, communities, and ecological systems. Much of the future of computers in the 21st century will be told by how well programmers can take advantage of concurrency.

This book gently introduces the general reader to some of the basic principles and some of the fascinating results of computer science which involve interactions between computing devices (or processors on the same or different devices), so that the reader can get a feel of the nature of this exciting and interesting field called *distributed computing*. These fundamental principles and results, underlying the design of algorithms for distributed systems, are presented by comparing issues that arise when dealing with groups of computing devices to those that arise when a group of people has to share their resources and work as a team to solve various problems. The book is self-contained; no reliance is made on previous knowledge in computer science. In particular, *all* the figures in the book which include code segments can be skipped without loss of continuity.

1.2 THE INTERNET

The Internet is a vast collection of computer networks which are connected into a single huge network. It is used for the transport of data and messages across distances which can be anywhere from the same room to anywhere in the world. It provides an infrastructure for the use of E-mail, banking, commerce, education, entertainment, telecommunications, manufacturing, and social networks and enables the sharing of remote resources such as databases, files, discs, printers, and computational resources. It also enables several computers to solve problems together much faster than any computer can do alone.

Historically, the Internet was designed as a research network without the expectation that it would have a significant role in our daily lives. The scale and heterogeneity of the Internet have far surpassed all expectations. As the Internet continues to grow, more and more business-critical functions rely on its availability. The vast majority of communications traffic, including telephone, television, radio, business data, and government data, rely on an Internet infrastructure that is available and secure.

Many applications of large-scale computer networks, such as the Internet, require a high level of reliability and security, for example, an air traffic control system, spacecraft navigation systems, or an integrated corporate management system. As the system size increases, so does the need to design fault-tolerant applications, for the probability that the entire system functions correctly at any given time rapidly approaches zero. Such applications enable the system as a whole to continue to function despite the failure of a limited number of components.

Today's economy involves manufacturing, distributing, and retailing of goods. However, it also has to do with creating and disseminating information, for example, publishing books, filmmaking, etc. Future economy is likely to be dominated by information. Information is a representation of knowledge, and can be represented in two ways: analog—a book that you can hold in your hand; or digital—a book that is stored as a file in your computer. The *digital revolution* is about converting analog information to digital information and use computer networks such as the Internet to move the digital information around. Such networks are required to be able to move the information in large quantities, everywhere, cheaply, securely, and as fast as possible.

1.3   COMPUTERS WITH MULTIPLE PROCESSORS

A *processor* is the brain of the computer. It is a component in a computer that interprets and execute computer program instructions and processes data. Throughout the history of modern computing, application developers have been able to rely on improved processor design to deliver significant performance improvements while reducing costs at the same time. That is, as processors got faster so did the applications. Unfortunately, increasing difficulty with heat and power consumption of the new smaller and faster processors along with the limits imposed by quantum physics has made this progression increasingly more difficult.

Until a few years ago mainstream computers were built with a single processor only. This situation has changed, as it became more difficult to increase the (clock) speed of uniprocessor computers. Hence, all microprocessor companies have been forced to bet their futures on multiple processors (also called multicores[1]) which resides inside a single computer.

Essentially, all computer manufacturers are now offering a new generation of multiprocessor computers where a single computer includes several processors all executing concurrently, and interact and collaborate with one another. Several computer manufacturers have been building, for many years now, costly high-end computers where each computer includes many processors,[2] however relatively cheap multiprocessor computers are available today as mainstream computers and can be found in many homes.[3] The switch from uniprocessors to multiprocessors is a milestone in the history of computing, and researchers have the rare opportunity to re-invent some of the cornerstones of computing.

This fundamental change in computing architecture requires a fundamental change in how such computers are programmed. Writing a *concurrent* application for a multiprocessor computer that takes advantage of having multiple processors to increase speed and get better performance is much more challenging and complex than programming a uniprocessor computer, and requires an understanding of new basic principles. Much of the future of computers with multiple processors will be told by how well programmers can take advantage of the new concurrent computing architecture.

1.4   SYNCHRONIZATION

Computation on computer networks like the Internet and computation on a single multiprocessor computer have many aspects in common. The key issue in both cases is the need to understand how separate computers on the Internet or, similarly, separate processors within a single com-

---

[1]Multicore means multiple processors embedded on the same chip (i.e., on the same piece of semiconducting material).

[2]In mid-2007, IBM unveiled Blue Gene/P, the second generation of one of the most powerful supercomputers in the world. The Blue Gene/P supercomputer configuration is a 294,912-processor, 72-rack system harnessed to a high-speed, optical network. It is used for executing applications like hydrodynamics, quantum chemistry, molecular dynamics, climate modeling, and financial modeling.

[3]The multicore era for mainstream computers began in spring 2005 when Intel and AMD (followed the lead of IBM and Sun Microsystems) announced that their microprocessors would rely on multiple processors or cores, and introduced computers with two processors each (dual-core processors) which enable the execution of two programs in parallel.

puter, interact and synchronize with one another. Synchronization techniques are perceived as essential to design and support the working activities of groups of computers and processors.

Many of our daily interactions with other people involve synchronization. You and your spouse may have to synchronize on who will buy the groceries, empty the garbage can, take the kids to school, which one of you will be the first to take a shower (assuming you only have one shower at home), will take the car, or use the single computer you have. Assume that you have a cat and your neighbor has a dog and you and your neighbor are sharing a yard, then you and your neighbor might want to coordinate to make sure that both pets are never in the yard at the same time.

In these examples, synchronization is used to ensure that only one participant (and not both) will take a specific action at a given time. Another type of synchronization has to do with cooperation. You and your spouse might need to move a heavy table together to its new location (it is too heavy for just one person). A classical example of cooperation is for two camps of the same army to decide on the exact time for a coordinated attack on the enemy camp.

We point out that the use of the term *synchronization* in computer science is slightly more general than its use in standard English. The following quote from the Oxford dictionary explains this point, "The use of *synchronize* to mean *coordinate* or *combine* as in *'We must synchronize our efforts'* is considered incorrect by some people and should be avoided in standard English." In computer science, synchronization also means coordination. That is, synchronization between processors is classified as either contention or coordination.

1.5   WHY IS SYNCHRONIZATION DIFFICULT?

All the above examples for synchronization between people have similar examples for synchronization between computers. Synchronization is needed in all systems and environments where several processors can be active at the same time. Without proper synchronization, the integrity of the data may be destroyed if two computers update a common file at the same time, and as a result, deposits and withdrawals could be lost, confirmed reservations might have disappeared, etc. However, while achieving synchronization between humans is sometimes relatively easy, achieving synchronization between computers is challenging and difficult. The reason is that most computers communicate with each other in a very restricted way.

While humans can see and hear each other, computers, and computing devices, in general, can in most cases only read and write. So, one computer can write a note (or send a message) that the other computer will later read, but they cannot see each other. To understand the difficulty with this type of restricted communication, the next two chapters examine several simple two-person interactions where communication is restricted either to writing and reading of notes or to sending and receiving of messages.

1.6   ALGORITHMS AND PROGRAMS

The notion of an algorithm is a central notion in computer science. An algorithm is just the recipe upon which a problem is solved. It was originally used in the context of solving mathematical problems. Euclid, the famous Greek mathematician, invented sometime between 400 and 300 B.C., an algorithm for finding the greatest common divisor of two possible integers. For example, the greatest common divisor of 18 and 27 is 9. This algorithm is considered to be the first non-trivial mathematical algorithm ever devised.

The word algorithm is derived from the name of the Persian mathematician Mohammed al-Khowârizmî, who lived in Baghdad during the 9th century. Al-Khowârizmî laid out the basic algorithms for adding, multiplying, and dividing numbers, and for extracting square roots. On a computer, an algorithm is expressed as a computer program which specifies, in the exact syntax of some programming language, the computation one expects a computer to perform. A recipe for preparing a cake, which prescribes the activities needed for preparing the cake, is also an algorithm. Such a recipe can be expressed in many different natural languages.

A plan or a strategy for winning in a game or solving a puzzle is also an algorithm. Thus, throughout the book, we shall use the terms, an algorithm, a plan, a strategy, or a solution, interchangeably. In most chapters of the book, we explain fundamental concepts which involve concurrency and synchronization between computers, by examining situations and solving problems which relate to interactions between people where communication is restricted in various ways. Thus, we shall use the terms a plan or a solution, more often than we shall use the term an algorithm.

1.7   CONCURRENT AND DISTRIBUTED ALGORITHMS

A concurrent or distributed algorithm is the recipe upon which a problem is solved by more than just one computing element. Finding the largest number in a set of numbers by first dividing the set into two subsets, using two processors to find the maximum number in each subset, and then comparing these two numbers, is an example of a simple concurrent algorithm. (Such an algorithm should also specify how to find the maximum in each subset.)

The term distributed algorithms refers to algorithms where the computing elements are physically far away from each other and communicate by sending and receiving messages (as done on the Internet). The term concurrent algorithms refers to algorithms where the computing elements are physically very close to each other and communicate by reading from and writing to shared memory locations (as done inside a multiprocessor computer). In the field of distributed computing, both types of algorithms are studied.

When a processor executes a computer program (such as a web browser), the execution itself is called a *process*. A process runs on a processor, which is the physical hardware. The physical location of the different processes or processors—we shall use the terms interchangeably—

involved in a single concurrent activity can be anywhere from the same computer to different computers anywhere in the world.

There are two main technological underpinnings of the fascinating rapid developments of computer networks and multiprocessor computers. The first is, of course, the advances in the design of faster hardware. The second is the development of efficient concurrent and distributed algorithms for supporting complex interactions between processors and computers. This book tells the story of the development of such algorithms. It is a fascinating story!

1.8   IMPOSSIBILITY RESULTS

In addition to the study of concurrent and distributed algorithms, the field of distributed computing also explores the inherent limitations of distributed systems: what problems cannot be solved in particular systems. Identifying features of a specific distributed system architecture that make it inadequate for solving certain problems is crucial for the design of better systems which can overcome such limitations.

Impossibility results help us understand the crucial limitations of real systems, why certain systems are (computationally) weak while others are powerful, when should we stop looking for a solution for a given problem, and how to adjust a problem statement or a system model to overcome an impossibility result.

Impossibility results usually depend on assumptions about: how the computing elements communicate with one another, what kinds of failures may occur, or whether randomization can be used. Such results are usually hard to prove.

Through the book, we will introduce and discuss some of the most fundamental impossibility results of distributed computing. We will highlight the insights gained from these results so that the reader can understand and appreciate their utmost importance.

1.9   CHAPTER NOTES

In 1968, Edsger Wybe Dijkstra, one of the most influential members of computing science's founding generation, published his famous paper "Co-operating Sequential Processes" [14], that originated the field of concurrent programming. A few concepts and results from Dijkstra's papers are covered in Chapters 2 and 7.

The Internet traces its beginning back to the early 1960s. At that time several research groups had invented a new technique, called packet switching, to transmit information as an efficient and robust alternative for circuit switching which is the transmission method used by the telephone network. Packet switching is the transmission method used today by the Internet. James F. Kurose and Keith W. Ross' excellent book *Computer Networking: A Top-Down Approach* explains and uses the Internet's architecture and protocols as primary vehicles for studying fundamental computer networking concepts [31].

In 1995, Gordon Moore published an article predicting exponential growth in the density of transistors in integrated circuits [37]. Since then, this prediction, known as "Moore's Law," went on to become a self-fulfilling prophecy. Moore's Law has become actual fact, with the doubling of transistor density every 18 months, as well as exponential growth in clock rates. However, due to inherent limitations imposed by the laws of physics, this exponential growth of the computing power of uniprocessors has to decline. The constraints of heat dissipation due to high-power consumption by fast uniprocessors have forced chip manufacturers to develop multicore architectures, where increases in throughput are achieved by packaging multiple cores embedded on the same chip which resides inside a single multiprocessor computer.

CHAPTER 2

One Loaf of Bread, Please

In many distributed systems, sometimes there is a need to ensure that two things will *not* happen at the same time. We use the *too much bread* problem to demonstrate the difficulty involved in such a type of synchronization when communication is restricted to sending and receiving messages.

2.1 THE TOO MUCH BREAD PROBLEM

Alice and Bob are sharing an apartment. They have decided that at any time they will try to have *precisely one* loaf of bread in the kitchen. Let's assume that Alice arrives home in the afternoon, and finds that there is no bread. So, she leaves for the bakery to buy bread. After she leaves, Bob arrives, he also finds that there is no bread and goes to buy bread. In the end, each one of them buys a loaf of bread, and they end up with too much bread. So, Alice and Bob are looking for a solution to ensure the following.

1. *Only one person buys a loaf of bread, when there is no bread.*
2. *Someone always buys a loaf of bread, when there is no bread.*

A solution in which only Bob is responsible for buying bread is not acceptable. In such a solution, there is a scenario where Alice arrives home and finds that there is no bread, and waits forever for Bob to show up. A proper solution should ensure that, when there is no bread, someone always buys bread even if only one person shows up.

Alice and Bob cannot see each other, and they communicate only by sending each other short text messages. It is assumed that a message that is sent is never lost and arrives immediately to its destination. However, between the time Alice finishes checking whether she has received a message and starts sending a message, Bob may send her a message.

2.2 APPLICATIONS

To see the corresponding synchronization problem for computing systems, replace *a loaf of bread* in the above example with a *file*, and let Alice and Bob be the names of two computers that are trying to avoid updating a shared file at the same time. As already mentioned in Chapter 1, without proper synchronization, the integrity of the data may be destroyed if two computers update a common file at the same time, and as a result, deposits and withdrawals could be lost, confirmed reservations might have disappeared, etc. Alice and Bob which communicate only by

PROGRAM FOR ALICE:

```
1 if (no B) {
2      if (no bread) {
3            send acquire
4            buy bread
5            send release
6      }
7 }
```

PROGRAM FOR BOB:

```
1 if (no A) {
2      if (no bread) {
3            send acquire
4            buy bread
5            send release
6      }
7 }
```

Figure 2.1: The code for the first incorrect attempt. The statement "if (no A)" means if Alice is not present, and the statement "if (no B)" means if Bob is not present.

sending text messages, correspond to computers which communicate by sending and receiving messages.

More generally, concurrent access to shared resources (like files, printers, memory locations, data structures) shared among several processes must be synchronized to avoid interference between conflicting operations. *Locks* are the de facto mechanism for concurrency control on concurrent resources: each resource is protected by a lock, a processor accesses a resource only after acquiring the lock protecting the resource, after which the processor is guaranteed exclusive access to that resource, once the processor completes its operation it releases the lock, enabling another waiting processor to access that resource. An algorithm that solves the too much bread problem is actually an implementation of a lock for two processes.

2.3   FIRST ATTEMPT

Alice and Bob have discussed the situation and agreed that to synchronize their actions they would communicate by sending two type of text messages: *acquire* (an attempt to acquire permission to buy bread) and *release* (giving up permission to buy bread). To simplify the presentation we will use the following conventions: We say the following.

- *Alice is present*, if the last message Bob has received from Alice is *acquire*.

- *Bob is present*, if the last message Alice has received from Bob is *acquire*.

By using these messages, Alice and Bob came up with the following solution.

Alice: *When Alice arrives home, she does the following: If she finds that Bob is not present and that there is no bread, she sends the message acquire, buys a loaf of bread, puts it on the kitchen table, and sends the message release.*

PROGRAM FOR ALICE:	PROGRAM FOR BOB:
1 send *acquire*	1 send *acquire*
2 **if** (no B) {	2 **if** (no A) {
3 **if** (no bread) {buy bread}}	3 **if** (no bread) {buy bread}}
4 send *release*	4 send *release*

Figure 2.2: The code for the second incorrect attempt.

Bob: *When Bob arrives home, he does the following: If he finds that Alice is not present and that there is no bread, he sends the message acquire, buys a loaf of bread, puts it on the kitchen table, and sends the message release.*

For readers familiar with basic programming notations, we give in Figure 2.1 the code for the first attempt to solve the problem. This and the other code segments in this chapter can be skipped without loss of continuity. In the solution, the statement "if (no A)" means if Alice is not present, and the statement "if (no B)" means if Bob is not present.

Well, the problem with this solution is that both Alice and Bob might buy bread. To see that, assume that they arrive home at the same time and recall that they cannot see each other. Now, Alice finds that Bob is not present and that there is no bread, and before she sends a message to Bob, Bob finds that Alice is not present and that there is no bread. Thus, both will send the message *acquire* and will go to buy bread ending up with "too much bread".

2.4   SECOND ATTEMPT

To resolve the above problem Alice and Bob slightly modified their previous solution.

Alice: *As soon as Alice arrives home, she sends the message acquire. Only then she checks, and if she finds that Bob is not present and that there is no bread, she buys a loaf of bread, puts it on the kitchen table, and sends the message release. Otherwise, if she finds that Bob is present, she sends the message release, and does nothing (until the day after, when she tries again).*

Bob: *As soon as Bob arrives home, he sends the message acquire. Only then he checks, and if he finds that Alice is not present and that there is no bread, he buys a loaf of bread, puts it on the kitchen table, and sends the message release. Otherwise, if he finds that Alice is present, he sends the message release, and does nothing (until the day after, when she tries again).*

The code for the second attempt appears in Figure 2.2.

Well, this time Alice and Bob might end up with no bread at all! To see that, assume that they arrive home at the same time. Since it is assumed that they cannot see each other, each one

PROGRAM FOR ALICE:	PROGRAM FOR BOB:
1 send *acquire*	1 send *acquire*
2 **if** (no B) {	2 **while** (A) {skip}
3 **if** (no bread) {buy bread}}	3 **if** (no bread) {buy bread}
4 send *release*	4 send *release*

Figure 2.3: The code for the third incorrect attempt. The statement "while (A) {skip}" means wait until Alice is not present.

sends the message *acquire*. Then, each one sees that the last message received from the other one is *acquire*, and no one buys bread.

2.5   THIRD ATTEMPT

Next, we present a solution which correctly works *only* if we make a timing assumption about the relative *speed* of Alice and Bob. The algorithm for Alice is the same as in the previous solution.

Alice: *As soon as Alice arrives home, she sends the message acquire. Only then she checks, and if she finds that Bob is not present and that there is no bread, she buys a loaf of bread, puts it on the kitchen table, and sends the message release. Otherwise, if she finds that Bob is present, she sends the message release and does nothing (until the day after, when she tries again).*

Bob: *As soon as Bob arrives home, he sends the message acquire. Then, if he finds that Alice is present, he waits until Alice is not present (that is until the last message received from Alice is not acquire). Once Bob finds that Alice is not present, he checks if there is bread. If there is no bread, he buys a loaf of bread, puts it on the kitchen table, and sends the message release. Otherwise, if there is bread, he sends the message release and does nothing.*

The code for the third attempt appears in Figure 2.3. As before, "if (no B)" means if Bob is not present. The statement "while (A) {skip}" means wait until Alice is not present, that is, wait until the last message received from Alice is not *acquire*.

For the above solution to be correct, an assumption must be made about Bob's speed. Let's assume that Bob is waiting for Alice to send a *release* message. Then, we should assume that, between the time Alice sends a *release* message (line 7), and the next time she sends the message *acquire* the day after (line 1), Bob must find out that the last message sent by Alice is a *release* message. That is, we must assume that Bob will not go to sleep before Alice sends a *release* message and will wake up only after Alice sends the message *acquire* the day after, never noticing that Alice's last message is a *release* message. Without this assumption, Alice and Bob

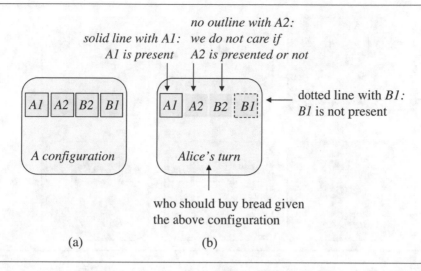

Figure 2.4: (a) A configuration where *A1, A2, B2*, and *B1* are all present. (b) Notations used in Figure 2.5.

might never buy bread. Such an assumption, where Alice and Bob are relatively slow, may be reasonable for humans. However, it is not reasonable for computers which are very fast.

2.6   FOURTH ATTEMPT: A CORRECT SOLUTION

Finally, we present a correct solution. Unlike the previous solution, it is symmetric: Alice and Bob behave similarly and hence have the same chance to go and buy bread. For this solution, *four* types of messages are used: *acquire1*, *release1*, *acquire2*, and *release2*. To simplify the presentation we will use the following conventions: We say the following.

- *A1 is present*, if Bob has received at least one *acquire1* message from Alice, and after the last *acquire1* message received, he has not received a *release1* message.

- *A2 is present*, if Bob has received at least one *acquire2* message from Alice, and after the last *acquire2* message received, he has not received a *release2* message.

- *B1 is present*, if Alice has received at least one *acquire1* message from Bob, and after the last *acquire1* message received, she has not received a *release1* message.

- *B2 is present*, if Alice has received at least one *acquire2* message from Bob, and after the last *acquire2* message received, she has not received a *release2* message.

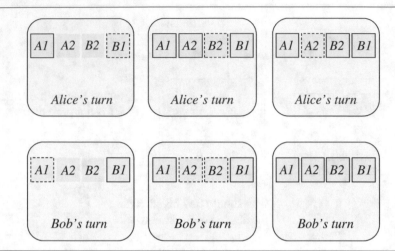

Figure 2.5: All the six possible configurations with *A1*, *A2*, *B2*, and *B1*.

A configuration is captured by deciding for each one of the symbols *A1*, *A2*, *B2*, and *B1* whether it is present or not present (see Figure 2.4). For any given configuration, it is either Alice's turn or Bob's turn (but not both) to buy bread.

At any point, as illustrated in Figure 2.5, if Alice finds that *B1* is not present, then it is Alice's responsibility to buy bread. If Bob finds *A1* is not present, then it is Bob's responsibility to buy bread. Otherwise, when both *A1* and *B1* are present, a decision is made according to the status of *A2* and *B2*. If both *A2* and *B2* are present or if neither of them is present then it is Bob's responsibility to buy bread, otherwise it is Alice's responsibility. More precisely, the solution is as follows.

Alice: *When Alice arrives home, she does the following.*

1. *First, she sends the message acquire1. Then, if B2 is present, she sends the message acquire2, otherwise she sends the message release2. By doing so, Alice gives priority to Bob in buying bread.*

2. *Then, she waits as long as the following two conditions hold: (1) B1 is present and (2) either both A2 and B2 are present or neither of them is present.*

3. *Once Alice finds that at least one of these two conditions is not satisfied, she checks if there is bread. If there is no bread, she buys a loaf of bread and puts it on the kitchen table.*

4. *Finally, she sends the message release1.*

Bob: *When Bob arrives home, he does the following.*

PROGRAM FOR ALICE:

```
1   send acquire1
2   if B2 {send acquire2}
3       else {send release2}
4   while (B1 and
5       ((A2 and B2) or
6           (no A2 and no B2)) ) {skip}
7   if (no bread) {buy bread}
8   send release1
```

PROGRAM FOR BOB:

```
1   send acquire1
2   if (no A2) {send acquire2}
3       else {send release2}
4   while (A1 and
5       ((A2 and no B2) or
6           (no A2 and B2)) ) {skip}
7   if (no bread) {buy bread}
8   send release1
```

Figure 2.6: The code for the fourth attempt. The statement "if B2" means if B2 is present; the statement "while (B1) {skip}" means wait until B1 is not present, etc.

1. *First, he sends the message acquire1. Then, if A2 is present, he sends the message acquire2, otherwise he sends the message release2. By doing so, Bob gives priority to Alice in buying bread.*

2. *Then, he waits as long as the following two conditions hold: (1) A1 is present and (2) either A2 or B2 are present (but not both).*

3. *Once Bob finds that at least one of these two conditions is not satisfied, he checks if there is bread. If there is no bread, he buys a loaf of bread and puts it on the kitchen table.*

4. *Finally, he sends the message release1.*

The solution will also work if Alice and Bob have a way to detect whether there is bread or not remotely. The code for the fourth attempt appears in Figure 2.6. In the solution, the statement "if B2" means if B2 is present; the statement "while (B1) {skip}" means wait until B1 is not present, etc.

This last solution is rather complicated, and it is not trivial to formally prove its correctness. The moral of this story is that even for such a simple problem it is challenging to come up with a correct solution when communication is done only by sending and receiving messages.

In reality, when computers need to be synchronized, much more difficult synchronization problems have to be solved. For example, there may be many participants (not just Alice and Bob), many resources (not just one loaf of bread), and under various assumption and requirements. A solution for three participants and two resources is presented in Chapter 10.

2.7   COMMUNICATING BY READING AND WRITING OF NOTES

We have assumed that Alice and Bob communicate only by sending each other short text messages, and we examined how the too much bread problem can be solved with this type of restricted communication.

As already mentioned, communicating devices usually communicate with each other by either (1) sending and receiving of messages or (2) reading from and writing to shared memory locations. So, let's turn our attention now to the reading and writing type of communication.

Assume that Alice and Bob cannot see each other and they communicate with each other only by writing and reading of notes. In particular, Alice cannot see that Bob is reading a note that she has written earlier. Inside their kitchen, there is a noticeboard, which is initially empty, on top of which they can leave notes and remove them later. How would we solve the problem with this type of restricted communication?

We point out that the noticeboard corresponds to a shared memory of a computer. Leaving and removing notes corresponds to writing into the shared memory, and reading of notes corresponds to reading from the shared memory. It is assumed that it is possible to atomically either read a note or leave/remove a note. However, between the time Alice finishes reading and starts updating the content of the noticeboard, Bob may access the noticeboard and possibly change its content.

Well, to solve the problem, we can essentially use the same correct solution (Solution 4) from page 13! We only need to give a different interpretation to some of the conventions used earlier. So, for this solution, *four labeled notes* are used: *A*1, *A*2, *B*1, and *B*2, and the following conventions are used: We say the following.

- *A1 is present*, if there is a note labeled *A1* on the noticeboard.

- *A2 is present*, if there is a note labeled *A2* on the noticeboard.

- *B1 is present*, if there is a note labeled *B1* on the noticeboard.

- *B2 is present*, if there is a note labeled *B2* on the noticeboard.

As before, a configuration is captured by deciding for each one of the four labeled notes *A1, A2, B2*, and *B1* whether it is present or not present (see Figure 2.4).

Now in the code for Alice in Solution 4, we substitute: send *acquire1* with leave note *A*1, send *acquire2* with leave note *A*2, send *release1* with remove note *A*1, and send *release2* with remove note *A*2.

Similarly, in the code for Bob in Solution 4, we substitute: send *acquire1* with leave note *B*1, send *acquire2* with leave note *B*2, send *release1* with remove note *B*1, and send *release2* with remove note *B*2.

This is it! With these modifications to Solution 4, we get a new correct solution for the too much bread problem assuming that Alice and Bob communicate with each other only by writing and reading of notes.

2.8   CHAPTER NOTES

The too much bread problem is an adaptation of the mutual exclusion problem to a model where communication is done only by sending and receiving messages. The correct solution we have presented for this problem, Solution 4, is an adaptation of an algorithm that was developed by J.L.K. Kessels for the mutual exclusion problem [30]. Kessels' algorithm itself is an adaptation of a mutual exclusion algorithm due to Gary Peterson [39]. Mutual exclusion algorithms were first introduced by Edsger W. Dijkstra in [13]. Since then, numerous implementations of such algorithms have been proposed. A book by Michel Raynal includes a collection of many early algorithms for mutual exclusion [44]. Detailed coverage of the topic of mutual exclusion can be found in [48].

Edsger W. Dijkstra (May 11, 1930–August 6, 2002) was a Dutch computer scientist who received the Turing Award in 1972. "For fundamental contributions to programming as a high, intellectual challenge; for eloquent insistence and practical demonstration that programs should be composed correctly, not just debugged into correctness; for illuminating perception of problems at the foundations of program design" [Extract from the Turing Award Citation]. The Turing Award is generally recognized as the highest distinction in computer science and the "Nobel Prize of Computing." It is named for Alan M. Turing, the British mathematician who articulated the mathematical foundation and limits of computing.

Dijkstra's fundamental contributions cover diverse areas of computing science, including compiler construction, operating systems, distributed systems, sequential and concurrent programming, programming paradigm and methodology, programming language research, program design, program development, program verification, software engineering principles, graph algorithms, and philosophical foundations of computer science and computer programming. In [3], various aspects of Dijkstra's life are discussed, including sections about his scientific career, scientific contributions, working style, opinions, lifestyle, and legacy.

2.9   SELF REVIEW

Questions:

1. As pointed out in Section 2.1 (page 9), a correct solution must satisfy the following two requirements: (1) only one person buys a loaf of bread, when there is no bread, and (2) someone always buys a loaf of bread, when there is no bread.

    (a) Does the first attempt solution in Section 2.3 (page 10) satisfy any of these requirements?

    (b) Does the second attempt solution in Section 2.4 (page 11) satisfy any of these requirements?

    (c) Does the third attempt solution in Section 2.5 (page 12) satisfy any of these requirements?

2. In the correct solution (page 13), Alice and Bob first send the *acquire1* message, and only then check what is the current configuration and take proper action. Is the order of those two actions significant? That is, if the order of those two actions is replaced, would the algorithm still be correct?

3. In the correct solution (page 13), Bob waits as long as the following two conditions hold: (1) A1 is present and (2) either A2 or B2 are present (but not both). Why can Bob not simply check these two conditions only once, and if both hold, conclude that Alice will buy a loaf of bread and go to sleep?

Answers:

1. (a) It satisfies requirement #2, but does not satisfy requirement #1. (b) It satisfies requirement #1, but does not satisfy requirement #2. (c) It satisfies requirement #1, but does not satisfy requirement #2.

2. No. In such a case, it is possible that both Alice and Bob will buy bread at the same time. To see why this claim is valid, assume that the order of those two actions is replaced (that is, line 1 appears after line 3), and consider the following scenario: initially, no message is sent. Alice arrives home, checks and sees that there are no messages from Bob. Then, *before* she manages to send a message, Bob arrives. Bob also notices that there are no messages from Alice, and so he sends the messages *acquire2* and *acquire1*. He checks again, and since there are no messages from Alice, he goes and buys bread. Alice continues. She sends the message *acquire1* and then checks and finds that *B2* is present and *A2* is not, she also goes and buys bread.

3. Because Alice might be in the middle of executing Step 1, after sending the message *acquire1*. If at that point Bob checks the two conditions and goes to sleep, Alice will complete Step 1, gives priority to Bob in buying bread, and will get stuck in Step 2.

CHAPTER 3

A Tale of Two Lovers

In many distributed systems, sometimes there is a need to ensure that two things happen together or not at all. The *two lovers* problem, which again involves two-person interactions, demonstrates the difficulty of reaching such an agreement when communication is restricted to sending and receiving messages which can get lost.

3.1 THE TWO LOVERS PROBLEM

The problem is for two lovers to decide on the *exact time* for a meeting. The problem is described as follows.

> Two lovers have to coordinate a time for meeting at a romantic restaurant for dinner. If they simultaneously arrive at the restaurant, they are assured to end up marrying and live happily ever after. If only one arrives, their relationship will come to an end. As a result, neither lover will arrive without a guarantee that the other will arrive at the same time. In particular, neither lover will arrive without communicating first with the other.
>
> The lovers can communicate only by sending messages. However, every time a message is sent it stands some chance of getting lost.
>
> The problem is to find an algorithm that allows the lovers to coordinate a time for a meeting even though some messages may get lost.

To prevent a situation where both lovers, fearing that their relationship will come to an end, simply refrain from arriving, it is required that if everything goes smoothly and no message is lost, the lovers must be able to coordinate a time for a meeting. If enough messages are lost, however, the lovers may refrain from arriving, but both must do so.

3.2 APPLICATIONS

To see the corresponding synchronization problem for computing systems, consider two computers (the two lovers) that are trying to perform a database transaction over an unreliable communication line, and need to decide whether to commit or abort the transaction.

A specific example would be the problem of transferring $100 between two bank accounts which reside in different banks. Two clerks (the lovers), who are responsible for the accounts, need to update that balance in the two accounts simultaneously. They should do it, even though their computers are connected by an unreliable communication channel.

The difficulty of solving computer network problems when the communication channels are unreliable (i.e., the channels can lose messages) emphasizes how important a reliable communication channel is. One of the most important Internet protocols, called TCP, tries to establish (in software) a reliable communication channel between two endpoints over an unreliable physical communication channel.

3.3   A SURPRISING IMPOSSIBILITY RESULT

Neither lover will decide to arrive unless s/he is sure that the other will arrive with her/him. Let's assume that everything goes smoothly and the messages do not get lost. How long does it take the two lovers to coordinate a time for a meeting?

Let's call the two lovers Alice and Bob. If Alice decides to arrive at a certain moment in the future, she can send a message to alert Bob. Would this be enough? As the message could be lost on its way, Alice cannot be sure that Bob will arrive with her and hence will not try to arrive. Thus Bob, in his turn, has to send another message back to inform Alice that the message has been delivered. Would this be enough for them? Well, now Bob needs to know whether his message has been delivered, to make sure that he will not arrive alone. Hence, Bob will not try to arrive until his message is acknowledged.

To solve this problem Alice, when she gets the message from Bob, has to send another message back to inform Bob that the message has been delivered, and so on. This scenario will never bring enough information to Alice and Bob, and hence we reach the following surprising conclusion:

There is no solution for the two lovers problem!

The moral of this example is that even such an elementary problem cannot be solved when communication is unreliable. Hence, in certain cases, there is a need to either accept the fact that mistakes will sometimes happen or make stronger assumptions about the environment to be able to solve various synchronization problems (an example of such stronger assumptions can be found in Chapters 4 and 5). Accepting the possibility of a mistake while trying to reduce it to an acceptable degree, one of the lovers could send 20 messages, anticipating that the probability of all being lost is low. With this approach, one lover will arrive at the restaurant no matter what, and the second lover will come if any message is received.

3.4   FURTHER EXPLANATIONS

Here is a simple proof of the above surprising impossibility result. Assume that a solution to the two lovers problem exists. Among all such possible solutions, let P be a solution that, in scenarios where no message is lost, sends the minimum number of messages. Now, suppose the last message sent in P gets lost. Then either this message is useless or one of the lovers does not get a needed message. By the minimality of P, the last message is not useless so exactly one of the lovers does not arrive if the last sent message is lost. This means that P does not solve the problem as assumed. This contradiction proves that there is no solution to the two lovers problem.

In the two lovers problem, it is required that the lovers will arrive simultaneously to the restaurant. In practice, simultaneity might be too strong a requirement. A solution that guarantees that they arrive within a short time of each other may be entirely satisfactory. Nevertheless, even such weaker forms of coordination are unattainable if communication is unreliable.

So, if the problem is unsolvable how can we human agree on things? Well, we settle for the agreement being "sufficiently likely" or "beyond reasonable doubt" instead of "with absolute certainty." I am willing to meet you somewhere provided that the probability of you arriving is high enough. After all, missing a meeting does not always ends up in a broken relationship :)

3.5 CHAPTER NOTES

The problem and its impossibility proof were first published by E. A. Akkoyunlu, K. Ekanadham, and R. V. Huber in 1975 [2], where it is described in the context of communication between two groups of gangsters. This problem was given the name *the two generals paradox* and *the two generals problem* by Jim Gray in 1978 in [22]. An alternative (and more complicated) impossibility proof appears in [26]. The problem is mostly known under the name the *coordinated attack problem*.

E. A. Akkoyunlu, K. Ekanadham, and R. V. Huber described the problem as follows: "A group of gangsters are about to pull off a big job. The plan of action is prepared down to the last detail. Some of the men are holed up in a warehouse across town, awaiting precise instructions. It is absolutely essential that the two groups act with complete reliance on each other in executing the plan. Of course, they will never get around to putting the plan into action, because the following sequence of events is bound to take place:

1. A messenger is dispatched across town, with instructions from the boss.

2. The messenger reaches his destination. At this point both parties know the plan of action. But the boss doesn't know that his message got through (muggings are a common occurrence). So the messenger is sent back, to confirm the message.

3. The messenger reaches the boss safely. Now, everybody knows the message got through. Of course, the men in the warehouse are not aware that step 3 occurred, and must be reassured. Off goes the messenger.

4. Now the men in the warehouse too know that step 3 was successful, but unless they communicate their awareness... " [2].

Jim Gray described the problem as follows: "There are two generals on campaign. They have an objective (a hill) that they want to capture. If they simultaneously march on the objective they are assured of success. If only one marches, he will be annihilated. The generals are encamped only a short distance apart, but due to technical difficulties, they can communicate only via runners. These messengers have a flaw, every time they venture out of camp they stand some chance of getting lost (they are not very smart). The problem is to find some protocol that allows the generals to march together even though some messengers get lost" [22].

James Nicholas "Jim" Gray was an American computer scientist who received the Turing Award in 1998 "for seminal contributions to database and transaction processing research and technical leadership in system implementation." The Turing Award is generally recognized as the highest distinction in computer science and the "Nobel Prize of Computing." Jim Gray was born January 12, 1944; presumed lost at sea January 28, 2007; declared deceased May 16, 2012.

3.6   SELF REVIEW

Questions:

1. Suppose the only possible meeting times are either 21:00 or 22:00. Is the two lovers problem solvable in this case?

2. Is the two lovers problem solvable when it is required that the lovers must be able to coordinate a time for a meeting only when no message is lost, and in all other cases they both should not show up?

3. Let's consider a variation of the problem. The two lovers have realized that they do not need to agree on an exact time for the meeting, it is ok if their meeting times are sufficiently close. In other words, each should eventually choose a time, such that the two times are sufficiently close.

4. This question is for readers familiar with the details of the TCP protocol. Is it possible to solve the two lovers problem if there is a reliable TCP channel between the two lovers?

Answers:

1–3. No. The impossibility proofs in all three cases are the same as before.

4. No. TCP only guarantees reliable delivery with an *infinite* number of possible retries. Thus, the argument in the above impossibility proof regarding the last message still holds. In fact, TCP is not involved in reaching the same decision among two communication parties, as in the two lovers problem.

CHAPTER 4

A Night at the Movies

The problem of reaching an agreement between several computing devices is a fundamental coordination problem and is at the core of many algorithms for fault-tolerant distributed applications. It is expressed abstractly as the following agreement problem.

4.1 THE MOVIE AGREEMENT PROBLEM

A group of students has decided to go for a movie together. Each one of them has an opinion of what movie they should go to. The *movie agreement* problem is to design an algorithm in which all the students reach a common decision on which movie they should go to, based on their initial opinions.

A movie agreement algorithm is an algorithm that produces such an agreement. While various decision rules can be considered such as "majority agreement," the problem is interesting even where the final decision is only constrained when all students are unanimous in their initial opinions, in which case the decision must be the common opinion. More formally, the problem is defined as follows.

Each student in the group has an initial opinion of which movie they should go to, and each student must eventually decide on a name of a movie. A student may decide at most once. The students communicate only by sending each other short text messages. We will assume that a message that is sent is never lost and arrives correctly to its destination. Each student is able to send messages directly to every other student.

What complicates the situation is that one or more of the students may *drop* at any time. A student that drops simply stops participating in the algorithm *without* notifying anybody and goes home.

The agreement problem is for the students to find an algorithm that satisfies the following two requirements.

- *Agreement*: All the students that haven't dropped eventually decide on the same movie.

- *Validity*: The movie that the students decide on is the initial opinion of at least one of the students. (It may be the input of a student that has dropped.)

The algorithm must guarantee the agreement condition regardless of how many students drop during the algorithm. Furthermore, the fact that students drop cannot cause the other students to adopt a decision and go to a movie that no student suggested. In particular, if all students are unanimous in their initial opinions then they choose this common initial opinion.

We point out that the first requirement has two parts. This first is that all students that decide choose the same movie, and the second is that all the student that haven't dropped eventually make a decision.

4.2   APPLICATIONS

To see the corresponding problem for computing systems, think of the students as computers (or processes) and of a student that drops as a malfunctioning computer that fails to respond (but never responds incorrectly). Such a failure is called crash failure or fail-stop failure. In the context of computing systems, the movie agreement problem is referred to as the consensus problem or the agreement problem.

In distributed systems, things fail. You can never count on anything being reliable. Software may have bugs, hardware and network connections can break, and messages can get lost. This means that it is never safe to rely on one copy of anything because that copy might become unavailable due to a failure. So, there is a need to keep multiple copies, and at any time those copies need to be consistent. That is, those copies need to *agree* on their contents. How can you make sure that the copies are consistent? The answer is using an agreement algorithm. Once you solved agreement, you solved the problem of how to build a distributed system that is more robust than any of its components.

Google achieves fault-tolerance of their databases through replications. A typical Google replication system consists of five replicas, running the same code, each running on a dedicated machine. An agreement algorithm, called Paxos, is used to keep replicas consistent in case of failures.

Microsoft has implemented a storage service that runs on the desktop computers of a large organization and provides the semantics of a central file server. This distributed file system replaces the physical security of a server in a locked room with the virtual security of cryptography, and uses fault-tolerant agreement-based replicated state machines.

Another application is maintaining consistency in a distributed network: Suppose that you have several sensor nodes monitoring the same environment. An agreement algorithm ensures robustness in the case where some of these sensors crash.

An important application of an agreement algorithm is the ability to use it, on-the-fly, for the election of a coordinator or a leader in an unreliable network. The leader can be used to compute and distribute some global information, for example, a spanning tree of the network. It can also initiate some global action, or decide who can use shared resources (such as databases, files, discs, printers, and computational resources) at any given time.

Reaching agreement also occurs in nature. Biological systems of ants, birds, bees, and bacteria reach agreement even when there is no leader. For example, the process where ants and bees decide on a location for a new nest to move into involves reaching agreement. We know they do it, but in most cases we do not know exactly how do they do it. The study of how these agreement building processes occur in nature has become a popular research topic recently in computer science.

4.3   A SURPRISING IMPOSSIBILITY RESULT

Achieving agreement is straightforward assuming that no student ever drops. All students can share their initial opinions and then all apply a uniform decision rule to the resulting set of initial opinions. That is, every student sends her initial opinion, of which movie to go to, to all students (including herself) and waits until she gets messages from all the other students. Then all the students apply the same uniform decision rule which, for example, can be: from the set of all initial opinions, choose the movie that appears first when the movies are arranged in alphabetical order.[1]

However, such a simple algorithm cannot tolerate even a single drop of a student, for its correctness depends on all processes obtaining the same initial set of opinions. That is, a student can no longer wait to receive messages from all other students since, in such a case, a student that drops can cause other students to wait indefinitely.

Assuming that at most one student drops, the next idea that comes to mind is for a student to wait until she receives messages from all but one other student. In such a case if a student succeeds in sending messages to some students but drops before sending to all students, then the other students may end up with different sets of initial opinions. In fact, even no student drops the students may end up with different sets of initial opinions. So, is there a way to "fix" the algorithm so that it can tolerate a single students' drop?

The surprising answer is that in an *asynchronous* system—a system where no assumption is made about the (relative) "speed" of the students (or of the messages)—there is no way to "fix" the algorithm. That is:

> *There is no movie agreement algorithm that can tolerate even a single student's drop, assuming that no assumption is made about the speed of the students or of the messages!*

The proof of the above impossibility result is rather complicated. The key insight in proving this result is that in asynchronous systems (as defined above) it is not possible to know that a student has dropped. That is, there is no way to distinguish between a student that has dropped and a student who takes steps very slowly or whose sent messages are very slow to arrive.

---

[1]Alphabetical order is a system whereby strings of characters are placed in order based on the position of the characters in the conventional ordering of an alphabet. To determine which of two strings comes first in alphabetical order, their first letters are compared. If they differ, then the string whose first letter comes earlier in the alphabet is the one which comes first in alphabetical order. If the first letters are the same, then the second letters are compared, and so on. If a position is reached where one string has no more letters to compare while the other does, then the first (shorter) string is deemed to come first in alphabetical order.

This impossibility result holds even if there are initially only two possible movies to choose between. Furthermore, it also holds when communication is done by reading and writing notes. (The communication model of reading and writing notes was explained in Chapter 2). In Section 4.5, we show how to solve the problem when additional assumptions are made about the speed of the students and of the messages.

4.4   A MORE GENERAL RESULT

The impossibility result from Section 4.3 is one of the most fundamental results in the area of distributed computing. Because of its importance, we state this results again using the standard computer science terms, as follows:

> *There is no agreement algorithm for two or more processors (or computers) that can tolerate*
> *even a single crash failure in an asynchronous system where communication is done either*
> *by sending messages or by reading and writing atomic registers.*

Let us explain all the notions that are mentioned in the above statement. As already explained, an *agreement* algorithm (also called consensus algorithm) is a plan (a strategy) for processors to reach a common decision based on their initial opinions. The decision value must be the initial opinion of some processor; thus, when all processors are unanimous in their initial opinions, the decision value must be the common opinion. An atomic register is a shared memory location that can hold a value, where a processor can atomically either read the value of the register or update the value of the register. However, between the time a processor finishes reading and starts writing, some other processor may access the register and possibly changes its value. A processor that *fails by crashing* is a processor that stops its execution. Finally, an asynchronous system is a system where no assumption is made about the (relative) "speed" of the processors and the messages.

4.5   AN ALGORITHM

The above impossibility result is for an asynchronous system. In this section, we assume that the students communicate with each other in "rounds." At the beginning of a round, each student may send messages to other students, and all the messages sent during a round arrive at their destinations by the end of this round. Computing systems in which communication is done in "rounds" are called *synchronous* systems. Below we present a movie agreement algorithm for such synchronous systems.[2] We assumed that all the students start participating in the algorithm at the same time.

Let n denotes the total number of students. Below we solve the problem assuming that at most t students may drop, where t is a number between 1 to n. The smaller t is, the faster the

---

[2]Practical computing systems are *not* synchronous! This very strong synchrony assumption allows for the design of relatively simple algorithms, and considered as a first step toward formulating practical solutions. See the Chapter Notes (Section 4.8) for a discussion of more practical solutions.

AGREEMENT FOR CRASH FAILURES WHERE $t + 1 \leq n$:
Algorithm for a student which initially supports $movie_i$

local variables v, *round*: integer

```
1   v ← movie_i; round ← 0
2   repeat at each round
3       round ← round + 1
4       send v to all the students
5       wait to receive all the messages sent during this round
6       v ← minimum (in alphabetical order) among all received values
        in this round, and the current value of v
7   until round = t + 1
8   decide on v
```

Figure 4.1: The code of the movie agreement algorithm.

students will be able to reach an agreement. The value of t is *a priori* known, so it can be used in designing the algorithm. It is possible to choose t to be n, in which case the algorithm will be able to tolerate any number of students' drops, however, in such a case it will take longer for the students to reach agreement (even if no student eventually drops).

The algorithm: The algorithm consists of exactly $t + 1$ rounds. In each round every student sends a message with her opinion (i.e., the movie she is suggesting) to all students (including herself), and waits until the end of the round to receive all the messages that were sent to her during the round. From the set of all messages that the student has received, in a given round, she chooses the movie that appears first when the movies are arranged in alphabetical order. Once she chooses the movie that appears first in alphabetical order, she continues to the next round supporting this movie as her new opinion. The algorithm terminates after $t + 1$ rounds.

It is shown below that at the end of round $t + 1$ all students have the same opinion. Furthermore, the movie that the students decide on is the initial opinion of at least one of them. (Notice that this implies that if all students have the same initial opinion, their final opinions are the same as the common initial opinion.) Interestingly, it is known that $t + 1$ rounds are also *necessary* for solving this problem.

The code is given in Figure 4.1. It can be skipped without loss of continuity.

4.6   FURTHER EXPLANATIONS

We show that the algorithm satisfies the *agreement* and *validity* requirements. We say that round k (where $1 \leq k \leq t + 1$) is *clean* if no student drops during round k. The first claim that we prove is the following.

> *Claim 1*: If round k is clean then at the end of round k all students choose the same movie as their opinion (and continue with this opinion to round $k + 1$).

To see why this claim is valid, consider the following proof. In a clean round every student sends her opinion at the beginning of the round (of which movie to go to) to all students (including herself), and by the end of the round the student receives messages from *all* the other students that have participated in the round. Thus, all the participating students in a clean round receive the same set of messages. Next, each student chooses the movie that appears first when the movies are arranged in alphabetical order, and thus all the students choose the same movie. The second claim below is even easier to prove.

> *Claim 2*: If at the beginning of round k all students have the same opinion then at the end of round k all students choose the same opinion and this opinion is the same as the opinion that they had at the beginning of round k.

To see why the second claim is valid, consider the following short proof. Since all the students have the same opinion, all the messages that are sent have the same content, and thus only one movie is suggested. Obviously, each student has only one movie to choose, and hence all student make the same choice.

We are now ready we show that the algorithm satisfies the *agreement* requirement. Since there are $t + 1$ rounds and up to t students may drop, there must be at least one clean round. By Claim 1, at the end of this clean round, all students choose the same opinion. In each round k that follows this clean round, since at the beginning of round k all students have the same opinion then, by Claim 2, at the end of round k all students choose the same opinion. Thus, after $t + 1$ rounds, all students decide upon the same movie.

Next, we show that the algorithm satisfies the *validity* requirement. Throughout the algorithm, the content of every message sent corresponds to some initial opinion of a student. Furthermore, each time a student chooses a movie to support, this movie must be the content of one of the messages the student has received. Thus, the movie that the students decide on must be the initial opinion of at least one of them.

4.7   HOW MANY ROUNDS ARE NEEDED?

In Section 4.5, an algorithm was presented that solves the agreement problem within $t + 1$ rounds assuming up to t students may drop. Are $t + 1$ rounds also necessary? Is there a faster agreement algorithm that always terminates after less than $t + 1$ rounds? According to the following fundamental result, there is no such algorithm.

In a synchronous message-passing system in which up to t students may drop, every (movie) agreement algorithm requires at least t + 1 rounds.

We point out that the above result means that for every agreement algorithm which can tolerate up to t students' drops, there must be at least one scenario (i.e., execution) which takes $t + 1$ rounds; it does not mean that *every* scenario must take $t + 1$ rounds.

4.8   CHAPTER NOTES

The agreement (consensus) problem was formally defined by Marshall Pease, Robert Shostak, and Leslie Lamport in [38]. The impossibility result that there is no agreement algorithm that can tolerate even a single crash failure in an asynchronous message-passing system was proved by Michael J. Fischer, Nancy A. Lynch, and Michael S. Paterson [20]. The two papers were awarded the prestigious Edsger W. Dijkstra Prize in Distributed Computing ([20] in 2001 and [38] in 2005).

A simple and elegant proof of the impossibility result for solving agreement in an asynchronous message-passing system in the presence of a single crash failure appeared in [46]. A simple and elegant proof, by Marcos K. Aguilera and Sam Toueg, that in a synchronous system with up to t crash failures solving agreement requires at least $t + 1$ rounds, appeared in [1]. A beautiful proof, by M.C. Loui and H. Abu-Amara, of an impossibility result for solving agreement in an asynchronous shared memory system which supports only atomic read/write registers in the presence of a single crash failure, appeared in [35].

The impossibility result for agreement from Section 4.4 is a special case of an impossibility result for the k-set agreement problem (also called k-set consensus). The *k-set agreement* problem for n processors is to find a solution where each processor starts with an input value from some domain and must choose some participating process' input as its output. All n processors together may choose no more than k distinct output values. The 1-set agreement problem is the familiar agreement problem. The following impossibility result generalizes the impossibility result for agreement: For any $k \geq 1$, there is no solution for the k-agreement problem for $k + 1$ or more processors (or computers) that can tolerate k crash failures in an asynchronous system where communication is done either by sending messages or by reading and writing atomic registers. The problem was defined by Soma Chaudhuri in [12]; the impossibility result was proved in [7, 28, 45].

As already mentioned, algorithms for synchronous systems, in which communication is done in "rounds," are not practical. Algorithms for asynchronous systems, where no assumption is made about the relative speed of the participating processes, are practical and operate properly in any system. However, this comes at the cost of efficiency and sometimes even solvability.

One solution is to design *time-resilient* algorithms. The appeal of time-resilient algorithms, which are also called *indulgent* algorithms, lies in the fact that when they are executed in an asynchronous system, they "lie in wait" for a short period of time during which certain timing constraints are met, and when this happens these algorithms take advantage of the situation and efficiently complete their mission [24, 25, 47]. Such a time-resilient agreement algorithm that is widely used by companies like Google, Microsoft, and Amazon, is the Paxos algorithm [32].

4.9   SELF REVIEW

Questions:

1. Is the validity requirement that "the movie that the students decide on is the initial opinion of at least one of them" equivalent to the requirement that "if all students are unanimous in their initial opinions then they must decide on this common initial opinion"?

2. Recall that it is assumed that *at most t* students may drop. Assume that it is never the case that exactly one student drops in a single round. That is, either in a given round no student drops or in a given round at least two students drop. Would the algorithm be correct if the number of rounds is $t/2 + 1$ instead of $t + 1$?

3. Let n be the number of students. Would the algorithm be correct, for *any* value of $0 \leq t \leq n - 1$:

    (a) if the number of rounds is n instead of $t + 1$?
    (b) if the number of rounds is $n - 1$ instead of $t + 1$?

4. Consider a synchronous message-passing system in which at most t students may drop, and after a student drops the student stops participating in the algorithm.

    (a) Assume that in a round, a dropped student either sends all its messages or none. Under this assumption, design an algorithm that solves agreement with as few rounds as possible.

    (b) Assume that in a round, a dropped student either sends all its messages, all its messages except one or none. Under this assumption, design an algorithm that solves agreement with as few rounds as possible.

    (c) Assume that in a round, a dropped student either sends all its messages, *only one* message or none. Under this assumption, design an algorithm that solves agreement with as few rounds as possible.

Answers:

1. No. Assuming the number of movies may be greater than 2, the former requirement is stronger. The later requirement enables the students to decide on a movie which is not the initial opinion of any of them.

2. Yes, since $t/2 + 1$ rounds are enough to guarantee that there is a clean round.

3. Yes, in both cases.

4. (a) One round suffice, the first round of the original algorithm. In this single round, every student sends a message with her opinion (i.e., the movie she is suggesting) to all students (including herself), and waits until the end of the round to receive all the messages that were sent to her during the round. From the set of all messages that the student has received she chooses the movie that appears first when the movies are arranged in alphabetical order.

   (b) $\min(2, t + 1)$ rounds suffice for every $t \geq 0$. In the first round, every student sends a message with her opinion to all students and waits until the end of the round to receive all the messages that were sent to her during the first round. In the second round, from the list of movies that were received in the first round (including her own), every student sends the movie that appears first to all students and waits until the end of the second round to receive all the messages that were sent to her. From the set of all messages that the student has received she chooses the movie that appears first.

   (c) $\min(2, t + 1)$ rounds suffice for every $t \geq 0$. In the first round every student sends a message with her opinion to all students and waits until the end of the round to receive all the messages that were sent to her during the first round. In the second round, each student sends *all* that she got in the first round (in one big message) to all other students and waits until the end of the second round to receive all the messages that were sent to her. Now each student that has not dropped knows who are all the students that dropped during the first round, and chooses the movie with the "smallest" name suggested by a student that did not drop during the first round.

CHAPTER 5

The Fall of the Byzantine Empire

Reliable computing systems must handle malfunctioning components that give conflicting information to different parts of the system. The problem of coping with this type of failure is expressed abstractly as the *Byzantine Generals Problem*, which is also known under the name *Byzantine Agreement*.[1]

5.1 THE BYZANTINE GENERALS PROBLEM

There is a group of generals of the Byzantine army camped with their troops around an enemy city. After observing the enemy, each general makes his own opinion about the required plan of action: either to attack or to retreat. Communicating only by sending messages using messengers, the generals must agree upon a common battle plan, namely, either all of them attack or all retreat. However, one or more of them may be traitors who will try to confuse the others.

The problem is for the generals to find an algorithm that satisfies the following two requirements.

- *Agreement*: All loyal generals decide upon the same plan of action: either to attack or to retreat.

- *Validity*: If all the loyal generals have the same initial opinion then they must agree on that opinion.

The loyal generals will all do what the algorithm says they should, but the traitors may do anything they wish. The algorithm must guarantee the agreement condition regardless of what the traitors do. Furthermore, the traitors cannot cause the loyal generals to adopt a bad plan—a plan that no loyal general supports.

It is assumed that the content of a message is entirely under the control of the sender, so a traitorous sender can transmit any possible message. However, it is assumed that communication is reliable. That is, we make the following three assumptions.

1. Every message that is sent is delivered correctly.

---

[1]It is recommended to read Chapter 4 before reading Chapter 5.

2. The receiver of a message knows who sent it.

3. The absence of a message can be detected.

The first two assumptions prevent a traitor from interfering with the communication between two other generals, since he cannot interfere with the messages they do send, and he cannot confuse their intercourse by introducing spurious messages. The third assumption will foil a traitor who tries to prevent a decision by simply not sending messages. Furthermore, it is assumed that each general is able to send messages directly to every other general. Because of the third assumption, when a traitor does not send a message, the general that is supposed to get it will detect that fact and may behave as if some default message is received from the traitor. Thus, from now on, we may assume that a traitor never tries not to send a message.

At first glance, the Byzantine Generals Problem seems deceptively simple to solve and utterly useless. In fact, it is hard to solve and extremely useful. To show that the problem is hard, consider a naive algorithm where all generals send out their opinions to each other, and then each general decides on the opinion that it received from the majority of other generals (for simplicity, assume that the number of generals is odd). This algorithm is incorrect because the traitors can send different messages to different generals. In particular, when the vote is close, the traitors can make one loyal general commit to attack and another loyal general commit to retreat.

5.2 APPLICATIONS

To see the corresponding problem for computing systems, think of the traitors as malfunctioning computers that give conflicting information to the correct computers. One way to implement a reliable computer system is to use several computers to compute the same result, and then to perform a majority vote on their outputs to obtain a single value. In such a case the correct computers will vote for the same result. This is true for protecting against a *Byzantine failure*—the strongest type of failures—by using redundant computing to increase the reliability.

Aircraft systems (such as the Boeing 777 Aircraft Information Management System), spacecraft navigation systems (such as the SpaceX Dragon flight system), the NASA Crew Exploration Vehicle, and distributed file systems (such as Microsoft Farsite storage service) are examples of systems which consider Byzantine fault tolerance in their design.

Byzantine agreement is essential for the implementation of *blockchain* which is a cryptography technology for implementing a distributed ledger. A distributed ledger is a tamperproof sequence of data that can be read and augmented by everyone. Distributed ledgers secure all kinds of traditional transactions, such as payments and asset transfers, in the exact order in which they occur. They also enable new transactions such as cryptocurrencies (Bitcoin for example) and smart contracts. Distributed ledgers stand to revolutionize the way a democratic society operates by removing intermediaries and thus providing a new paradigm for trust.

One way to reduce the cost of achieving reliability in computer systems and networks is to make assumptions about the type of failure that may occur. For example, as done in Chapter 4, it can be assumed that a computer may fail to respond but will never respond incorrectly. However, when extremely high reliability is required, such assumptions cannot be made, and the full expense of a Byzantine Generals Solution is required.

5.3   A SURPRISING RESULT

We have already noticed in Chapter 4, that there is no agreement algorithm that can tolerate even a single *crash* failure in an *asynchronous* message-passing system. Recall that asynchrony means that no assumption is made about the speed of the generals (processors) or of the time it takes to deliver a message. Since a Byzantine failure is more severe than a crash failure, it follows that there is no Byzantine agreement algorithm that can tolerate even a single traitor in an asynchronous message-passing system.

So, to overcome this difficulty, assume that it takes a general almost no time to decide which messages to send next and messages arrive immediately at their destination (such an assumption is called the *synchrony* assumption). We know from the presentation in Chapter 4, that under such an assumption there is a (movie) agreement algorithm that can tolerate any number of *crash* failures. Is this result true also from Byzantine failures? That is, is there a Byzantine agreement algorithm that can tolerate any number of traitors? The answer is negative. The following is known.

> Even if it takes a general almost no time to decide which messages to send and messages arrive immediately at their destination, there is no solution to the Byzantine Generals Problem unless *more than two-thirds* of the generals are loyal! In particular, with only three generals, no solution can work in the presence of a single traitor.

The proof of the above result is very complicated. This surprising impossibility result is another indication for the difficulty of solving the Byzantine Generals Problem.

5.4   AN ALGORITHM

Complicated solutions exist for solving the Byzantine Generals Problem assuming more than two-thirds of the generals are loyal. Below we solve the problem under a stronger assumption: the number of loyal generals exceeds thrice the number of traitors. That is, more than *three-quarters* of the generals are loyal. So, assume that there are at least ℓ ℓoyal generals and at most t $t$raitors, where $\ell > 3t \geq 0$. The value of t is *a priori* known, so it can be used in designing the algorithm.[2] To simplify matters, assume that the total number of generals, $\ell + t$, is odd.

---

[2]It is possible to choose ℓ to always be exactly $3t + 1$, in which case the algorithm will be able to tolerate any number of traitors as long as *three-quarters* of the generals are loyal; however, in such a case it will take longer for the loyal generals to reach agreement when the number of traitors, t, is much smaller than one quarter of the total number of generals.

Let the generals be numbered 1 through $\ell + t$. Generals communicate with each other in "phases." Each phase consists of two rounds of message transmissions. At the beginning of a round, each general may send messages to other generals and all the messages sent during a round arrive at their destinations by the end of this round.[3] All the generals start participating in the algorithm at the same time.[4]

> *The algorithm:* The algorithm consists of exactly $t + 1$ phases. In phase k, where $1 \leq k \leq t + 1$, in the first round every general sends his opinion (which is either *attack* or *retreat*) to all generals (including himself); in the second round, only general k sends the majority opinion he received in the first round (majority is well defined since $\ell + t$ is assumed to be odd) to all generals. If a general receives ℓ, or more, instances of the same opinion in the first round of phase k, he chooses this opinion (which is supported by ℓ generals) as his new opinion for the next phase; otherwise, he chooses the opinion received (from general k) in the second round of phase k and continues to the next phase supporting this opinion. The algorithm terminates after $t + 1$ phases.

It is shown below that at the end of phase $t + 1$ all loyal generals have the same opinion. Furthermore, if all loyal generals have the same initial opinion, their final opinions are the same as the (common) initial opinion. Since each phase of the algorithm includes two rounds, the round complexity of the algorithm is $2(t + 1)$ rounds. It is known that $t + 1$ rounds are necessary and sufficient for solving the problem, so this algorithm is not optimal. The code is given in Figure 5.1. It can be skipped without loss of continuity.

5.5 FURTHER EXPLANATIONS

It is shown below that the algorithm satisfies the *agreement* and *validity* requirements. We say that phase k is *clean* if general k is loyal. Let us denote by *majority.k* the majority opinion that general k has received (including his own opinion) in the first round of phase k.

> *Claim 1*: If phase k is clean then at the end of phase k all loyal generals choose the same opinion, and this common opinion is *majority.k*.

To see why this claim is valid, consider the following proof. By definition, general k received the value *majority.k* from more than half of the generals at the first round of phase k. Thus, general k received *majority.k* from more than a fourth of the loyal generals (at the first round of phase k). This implies that *every* loyal general received *majority.k* from more than a fourth of the loyal generals (at the first round of phase k). Thus, if a general received at least ℓ identical messages

---

[3]Recall the explanation from page 34, why we may assume that a traitor never tries *not* to send a message.

[4]Computing systems in which communication is done in "rounds" are called *synchronous* systems. Practical computing systems are *not* synchronous! This very strong synchrony assumption allows for the design of relatively simple algorithms, and considered as a first step toward formulating practical solutions. See the Chapter Notes of Chapter 4 for a discussion of that issue.

AGREEMENT FOR BYZANTINE FAILURES WHERE $t < n/4$:
Algorithm for a general with identifier $i \in \{1, ..., n\}$.

local variable v: integer

1    $v \leftarrow$ general i's initial opinion which is either *attack* or *retreat*
2   **for** $k = 1$ **to** $t + 1$ **do**
3   **round 1:** send v to all the generals (including yourself)
4   and receive messages from all the generals
5   **round 2: if** my identifier i equals k
6   **then** $v \leftarrow$ "majority value received in round 1";
7   send v to all the generals (including yourself)
8   **else** receive a value general k
9   **if** in round 1 you have received ℓ or more messages with the same value
10   (including your own)
11   **then** assign this value to v
12   **else** assign to v the value you have received in round 2
13 **end loop**
14 **decide** on v

Figure 5.1: The code of the Byzantine agreement algorithm. There are at least ℓ loyal generals and at most t traitors. The number of generals is $n = \ell + t$, and the generals are uniquely numbered 1 through n.

at the first round then the value of this messages must be *majority.k*, and hence the general will choose *majority.k* as his opinion at the end of round k. Furthermore, if a general received less than ℓ identical messages at the first round then he will choose *majority.k* as his opinion at the end of round k. This completes the proof of the first claim. The second claim below is much easier to prove.

> *Claim 2*: If at the beginning of phase k all loyal generals have the same opinion then at the end of phase k all loyal generals choose the same opinion and this opinion is the same as the common opinion that they had at the beginning of phase k.

To see why the second claim is valid, consider the following short proof. It was assumed that ℓ, the number of loyal generals, is more than *three-quarters* of the total number of generals. Let us denote by v the common opinion (i.e., *attack* or *retreat*) that all the loyal generals are assumed to have at the beginning of phase k. Each loyal general sends a message with the value v, and receives (at least) ℓ messages with the value v at the first round of phase k. Thus, following the algorithm, each loyal general chooses the value v at the end of phase k. This completes the proof of the second claim.

We are now ready to show that the algorithm satisfies the *agreement* requirement. Since there are $t + 1$ phases and only t traitors, there must be at least one clean phase. By Claim 1, at the end of this clean phase, all loyal generals choose the same opinion. In each phase k that follows this clean phase, since at the beginning of phase k all loyal generals have the same opinion then, by Claim 2, at the end of phase k all loyal generals choose the same opinion. Thus, after $t + 1$ phases, all loyal generals decide upon the same plan of action: either attack or retreat.

Next, we show that the algorithm satisfies the *validity* requirement. Assume that all the loyal generals have the same initial opinion, say v (v is either attack or retreat). By Claim 2, if at the beginning of phase k all loyal generals have the same opinion v, then at the end of phase k all loyal generals still have the same opinion v. Assuming that all the loyal generals have the same initial opinion v then by Claim 2, they will preserve this value and by the end of phase $t + 1$ all the loyal generals will still have the same opinion v. Finally, when not all the loyal generals have the same initial opinion, then both to attack and to retreat are legal decisions.

5.6 CHAPTER NOTES

The Byzantine Generals Problem originated from two seminal papers by Marshall Pease, Robert Shostak, and Leslie Lamport [38] and by Lamport, Shostak, and Pease [33]. These two papers contain upper and lower bounds for the case where more than *two-thirds* of the generals are loyal. The first paper was awarded the 2005 Edsger W. Dijkstra Prize in Distributed Computing. It is the second paper that coined the name *Byzantine Generals* for describing the problem and the fault model.

The Byzantine agreement algorithm presented in this chapter is due to Piotr Berman and Juan A. Garay [5]. The result that in a synchronous system with up to t Byzantine failures solving consensus requires at least $t + 1$ rounds was proved by Michael J. Fischer and Nancy A. Lynch in [18]. This result follows immediately from the much stronger result for crash failures discussed in Section 4.7 (page 28) [1].

The traitors' ability to lie is what makes the Byzantine Generals Problem so difficult. Let's assume that the generals can send unforgeable signed messages. More precisely, assume that: (1) a loyal general's signature cannot be forged, and any alteration of the contents of his signed messages can be detected; and (2) anyone can verify the authenticity of a general's signature. We make no assumptions about a traitorous general's signature. In particular, we allow a traitor's signature to be forged by another traitor, thereby permitting collusion among the traitors. It is interesting to note that when assuming unforgeable signed messages, the Byzantine Generals Problem is solvable for any number of traitors [33]. That is, in such a case, there is no need to assume that more than *two-thirds* of the generals are loyal.

The Byzantine Empire stood at the geographical and cultural center of the European and Middle-Eastern world for more than 1,000 years. From inception as the eastern half of the partitioned Roman Empire in the 4th century AD through to final disappearance in the 15th century—Byzantium played the role of an economic, political, and cultural superpower.

In his notes, Leslie Lamport discusses the reason for naming the problem, the Byzantine Generals Problem.

"The popularity of the dining philosophers problem[5] taught me that the best way to attract attention to a problem is to present it in terms of a story.

There is a problem in distributed computing that is sometimes called the Chinese Generals Problem,[6] in which two generals have to come to a common agreement on whether to attack or retreat, but can communicate only by sending messengers who might never arrive. I stole the idea of the generals and posed the problem in terms of a group of generals, some of whom may be traitors, who have to reach a common decision. I wanted to assign the generals a nationality that would not offend any readers. At the time, Albania was a completely closed society, and I felt it unlikely that there would be any Albanians around to object, so the original title of this paper was *The Albanian Generals Problem*. Jack Goldberg was smart enough to realize that there were Albanians in the world outside Albania, and Albania might not always be a black hole, so he suggested that I find another name. The obviously more appropriate Byzantine generals then occurred to me."

Leslie Lamport (born February 7, 1941) is an American computer scientist who received the Turing Award in 2013—"For fundamental contributions to the theory and practice of distributed and concurrent systems, notably the invention of concepts such as causality and logical clocks, safety and liveness, replicated state machines, and sequential consistency" [Extract from the Turing Award Citation]. The Turing Award is generally recognized as the highest distinction in computer science and the "Nobel Prize of Computing."

5.7   SELF REVIEW

Questions:

1. Is the validity requirement that "if all the loyal generals have the same initial opinion then they must agree on that opinion" equivalent to the requirement that "the plan that the generals agree on is the initial opinion of at least one of them?"

2. The question refers to the algorithm in Section 5.4. Recall that it is assumed that there are at least ℓ loyal generals and at most t traitors, where $\ell > 3t \geq 0$.

   (a) What is the smallest number m for which the following claim is correct: "If the initial opinions of at least m loyal generals is *attack* then at the end of phase $t + 1$ the final opinion (decision) of all the loyal generals is *attack*."

[5] Chapter 7, page 51.
[6] Chapter 3, page 22.

(b) Suppose that instead of assuming that $\ell > 3t$, it is assumed only that $\ell \geq 3t - 1$, and instead of running for $t + 1$ phases, the algorithm runs for k phases, where $t + 1 \leq k \leq n$, with the same decision rule. ($n = \ell + t$ is the total number of generals.) Is there a value of k for which the modified algorithm correct?

Answers:

1. Yes. Unlike the movie agreement problem (Chapter 4), in the Byzantine Generals Problem, there are only two possible opinions to choose from.

2(a) The smallest value for m that guarantees that *attack* will be chosen is $m = \ell$.

2(b) Incorrect for any value of k.

CHAPTER 6

Sightseeing in Paris

A central issue in distributed computing is how to coordinate the actions of various processors of a computing system. For such coordination, there is sometimes a need for the processors to choose between several possible alternatives. Coordination becomes even more difficult when there is no *a priori* agreement between the processors on names for the alternatives, and when some of the processors can stop functioning. The choice coordination problem highlights many of the difficulties inherent in situations.

6.1 THE CHOICE COORDINATION PROBLEM

The problem is for a group of tourists to decide between two meeting places for the beginning of a sightseeing tour: inside the Notre-Dame de Paris cathedral or inside the Louvre museum. The tourists may not communicate as a group, nor is there a central "authority" which will make the decision for them. The problem is described as follows.

> Each tourist carries a notepad on which s/he will write various numbers; outside each of the two potential meeting places is a noticeboard on which various messages will be written. Initially, the number 0 appears on all the notepads and on the two notice-boards. This should be interpreted as having all the notepads and the noticeboards initially blank.

> Each tourist *independently* decides which place to visit first, after which the tourist strictly alternates the visits between the two places.[1] At each visit s/he looks at the noticeboard there, and if it displays "here," the tourist concludes that this is the chosen meeting place and goes inside. If it does not display "here" it will display a number instead. The tourist, in one step without any interruption from other tourists, compares that number on the noticeboard with the one on the notepad then takes an action which may change the numbers on the noticeboard and the notepad.

> A solution for the choice coordination problem is an algorithm (i.e., a set of instructions that each tourist should follow) such that for every order in which the tourists start participating, eventually all tourists reach a common decision of entering the same place, without communicating directly with each other. The solution should be correct regardless of how many tourists show up and participate in the algorithm.

[1] The walking distance between the Notre-Dame de Paris cathedral and the Louvre museum is 1.6 km. It takes about 20 min walking, and 10 min cycling.

Furthermore, it should be correct even if any number of participating tourists decide at any point in time that they are not interested in the tour, stop participating and go back to the hotel.

Finally, the names of the two potential meeting places should not be used, in any way, when designing the algorithm. That is, each tourist calls the location s/he visits first, the first location, and calls the other location, the second location. In that sense, since each tourist *independently* decides which place to visit first, there is no *a priori* agreement between the tourist on the names for the two meeting places.

The agreement on a single choice is complicated by the fact that there is no *a priori* agreement on names for the two alternatives. That is, the requirements that each tourist decides independently which place to visit first and that the actual names of the two potential meeting places should not be used. This is the main difference between the choice coordination problem and the movie agreement problem from Section 4, in which there is *a priori* agreement on names for the alternatives. This last requirement enables to use a choice coordination algorithm to decide between any two potential meeting places, not just the Notre-Dame de Paris cathedral and the Louvre museum.

6.2   APPLICATIONS

A more concrete version of the problem associates a shared register with each alternative (i.e., each possible meeting place). All inter-process communication must be accomplished by writing in these registers. However, the registers do not have global names; the first register examined and the subsequent order in which registers are scanned may be different for each process. A special symbol must be written in exactly one register, and all correct processes must terminate pointing to this register. The efficiency of an algorithm is defined by the number of different symbols which may be written in the registers, and the running time—the number of visits.

A central issue in distributed computing is how to coordinate the actions of asynchronous processes. Coordination becomes even more difficult if as many as $n - 1$ of the n processes can fail. The choice coordination problem highlights many of the difficulties inherent in such wait-free situations.

Solutions to the problem thus lend insight into how to coordinate asynchronous actions. For example, in the course of a computation, k almost identical versions of a text are being generated, and the processes have to agree on one of these as the commonly used version. Thus, a choice coordination problem arises.

Choice coordination problems also occur in nature. Below we describe a zoological application. The mite of the genus *Myrmoyssus* parasites the ear membrane of moths of the family *Phaenidae*. If both ears of a moth are infected, it does not hear the sonar of bats that prey on it and is in greater danger of being devoured together with its colony of mites. The mites employ an ear-choice coordination algorithm involving chemical markings of trails. The ear-choice coordination algorithm is an example of choice coordination to decide which ear to infect.

6.3   A RANDOMIZED ALGORITHM

In some systems, termination cannot be guaranteed for certain. Instead, a slightly weaker property is mostly sufficient and appropriate: termination with probability 1. An example of having such a property is when tossing a fair coin, eventually heads will come up. In other words, the coin will turn up heads with probability 1. There are many applications in distributed systems of such a "coin flip," in particular for symmetry breaking. An algorithm which makes use of tossing a fair coin to make a decision is called a randomized algorithm. Since we are assuming that initially the number 0 appears on all the notepads and the two noticeboards, in order to break symmetry, we will need to use randomization (i.e., coin tossing).

The algorithm: *As already mentioned, each tourist decides independently which place to visit first, after which the tourist strictly alternates between the two places. At each visit the tourist compares the number on the noticeboard, denoted K, with the one on the notepad, denoted k, then taking one of the following actions.*

- *If "here" is written on the noticeboard, the tourist goes inside.*

- *If $k < K$, the tourist writes K on the notepad (erasing k), and goes to the other place.*

- *If $k > K$, the tourist writes "here" on the noticeboard (erasing K), and goes inside.*

- *If $k = K$, the tourist strictly increases K to the next higher odd number, and then flips a fair coin; if it comes up heads, the tourist increases it one further. The tourist then writes (the new) K on the noticeboard and the notepad (erasing k and the "old" K), and goes to the other place.*

The algorithm above terminates with probability 1, and on termination all tourists will be inside, at the same meeting place! The fascinating thing about this randomized algorithm is that it does not require knowing in advance the number of tourists nor does it require that the tourists have unique names of tourists. Furthermore, it is not required to assume that initially the numbers appearing on all the notepads are different. The code is given in Figure 6.1. This and the other code segment in this chapter can be skipped without loss of continuity. For two values x and y, R is the reflection function on $\{x, y\}$ if $x = R(y)$ and $y = R(x)$.

6.4   FURTHER EXPLANATIONS

We first explain why "here" cannot be written on both noticeboards. Let us assume to the contrary that at some point in time "here" was written on both noticeboards, and show that this assumption leads to a contradiction. Let Alice and Bob be two of the tourists. Clearly, neither Alice alone nor Bob alone wrote "here" on both noticeboards. For simplicity, let us call the two

A RANDOMIZED CHOICE COORDINATION ALGORITHM

shared   *Board*[*Notre-Dame*], *Board*[*Louvre*]: ranges over {integers ∪ {*here*}}, initially 0
local   *notepad*: integer, initially 0
         place: bit, ranges over {Notre-Dame,Louvre}
         s: bit, ranges over {0, 1}
         done: boolean, initially *false*
$R(\cdot)$ is the reflection function on {Notre-Dame,Louvre}

```
1   place ← a random element from {Notre-Dame,Louvre}// decide which place to visit
2   repeat                              // lines 3--10 are executed as one atomic step
3       if Board[place] = here then done ← true
4       elseif notepad < Board[place] then notepad ← Board[place]
5       elseif notepad > Board[place] then Board[place] ← here; done ← true
6       elseif notepad = Board[place] then
7           s ← a random element from {0,1}                        // flip a coin
8           if Board[place] is even then Board[place] ← Board[place] +1 + s
9           else Board[place] ← Board[place] +2 + s
10          notepad ← Board[place]
11      if done = false then place ← R(place)              // go to the other place
12  until done = true
13  if place = Notre-Dame then the meeting place is the Notre-Dame de Paris cathedral
14  else the meeting place is the Louvre museum
```

Figure 6.1: The algorithm for a tourist. It is not required to know in advance the number of tourists. The initial numbers that appear on all the notepads are the same.

noticeboards A and B, and assume that Alice wrote "here" on A, and Bob wrote "here" on B. Let α and β be the last numbers written on A and B, respectively. The last value Alice read when visiting B was greater than α. Since the numbers written on each noticeboard may only increase, it follows that $\alpha < \beta$. Since α is the greatest number written on A, it follows that all the numbers that Bob read when visiting A were less than β. However, in order to be able to write "here" on B, Bob must have read a number greater than β when visiting A. A contradiction. This explains why "here" cannot be written on both A and B.

Next, we explain why the algorithm terminates with probability 1. We show that, for any positive integer $m > 0$, the probability that a value greater than m will be written on a noticeboard before "here" is written, is at most $1/2^{m/2}$. Thus, as m goes to infinity, the probability that a value greater than m will be written before "here" goes to 0. The only way that a value greater than m is written is that at some point in time, say t, $m - 1$, or m is written on both noticeboards. For this to occur there must be times $t_1 < t_2 < ... < t_{m/2} = t$, such that: at time t_1 either 1 or 2 is written on both noticeboards, at time t_2 either 3 or 4 is written on both noticeboards, etc. Thus, $m/2$ times, independent coin flips on the two noticeboards must produce the same value. The probability of a single such event is $1/2$ and the probability of $m/2$ such repetitions is $1/2^{m/2}$.

6.5   A SIMPLE DETERMINISTIC ALGORITHM

Let's assume that symmetry is broken by assuming that initially, the number that appears on the notepad of each tourist is a unique number which is different from 0. This is like assuming that the tourists are not identical and have unique names. In such a case, it is possible to solve the problem without the need of tossing a fair coin. An algorithm which does not make use of coin tossing is called a deterministic algorithm. Assume that, initially the number 0 appears on the two noticeboards.

The algorithm: *As before, each tourist independently decides which place to visit first, after which the tourist strictly alternates between the two places. Each tourist visits the two places at most three times after which the tourist goes inside one of them. At each visit, the tourist compares that number on the noticeboard, denoted K with the unique number on the notepad, denoted k, then taking action as explained below.*

- *First visit: If "here" is written on the noticeboard, the tourist goes inside; otherwise, if $K = 0$, the tourist writes k on the noticeboard (erasing K), and goes to the other place; otherwise (when $K \neq 0$), the tourist writes K on the notepad (erasing k), and goes to the other place.*

- *Second visit: If "here" is written on the noticeboard, the tourist goes inside; otherwise, if $K = 0$ or $k < K$, the tourist writes "here" on the noticeboard (erasing K), and goes inside; otherwise (if $k > K$) the tourist goes to the other place.*

- *Third visit: If "here" is written on the noticeboard, the tourist goes inside; otherwise, the tourist writes "here" on the noticeboard (erasing K) and goes inside.*

The code is given in Figure 6.2. We explain why eventually "here" will be written on exactly one noticeboard, and thus all the tourists will go inside the same place. If some tourist completes the first two visits before all the other tourists start, s/he will write "here" during the second visit and all the other participating tourists will eventually see it without writing anything on the noticeboards. Similarly, if a tourist sees 0 during the second visit (which implies that each other tourist has completed at most one visit) the tourist will write "here" during the second visit and all the other participating tourists will eventually see it without writing anything on the noticeboards (since "here" was written). Otherwise, if some tourist writes the number i on one of the noticeboards, and another tourist writes the number j on the other noticeboard, then eventually "here" will be written only on the noticeboard on which $\max(i, j)$ is written.

A DETERMINISTIC CHOICE COORDINATION ALGORITHM

shared
      $Board[Notre\text{-}Dame]$, $Board[Louvre]$: ranges over {integers $\cup$ {$here$}}, initially 0
local $notepad$: integer, initially a *unique* number which is different than 0
      $place$: bit, ranges over {Notre-Dame,Louvre}
$R(\cdot)$ is the reflection function on {Notre-Dame,Louvre}

1     $place \leftarrow$ a random element from {$Notre\text{-}Dame,Louvre$}   `// decide independently`
                          `// first visit: lines 2--4 are executed as one atomic step`
2   **if** $Board[place] = here$ **then goto** done   `// meeting place is known`
3   **elseif** $Board[place] = 0$ **then** $Board[place] \leftarrow notepad$
4   **elseif** $Board[place] \neq 0$ **then** $notepad \leftarrow Board[place]$
5     $place \leftarrow R(place)$ `// go to the other place`
                          `// second visit: lines 6--7 are executed as one atomic step`
6   **if** $Board[place] = here$ **then goto** done   `// meeting place is known`
7   **elseif** $Board[place] = 0$ **or** $notepad < Board[place]$ **then** $Board[place] \leftarrow here$; **goto** done
8     $place \leftarrow R(place)$ `// notepad > Board[place], go to the other place`
                        `// third visit: line 9 is executed as one atomic step`
9   **if** $Board[place] \neq here$ **then** $Board[place] \leftarrow here$
10   **goto** done   `// meeting place is known`

11 done:
12   **if** $place = Notre\text{-}Dame$ **then** the meeting place is the Notre-Dame de Paris cathedral
13   **else** the meeting place is the Louvre museum

Figure 6.2: The algorithm for a tourist. Initially, the number that appears on the notepad of each tourist must be a unique number which is different than 0.

6.6   PERFECTIONISM, IT SEEMS, DOES NOT PAY!

How many different symbols are needed for solving the choice coordination problem? That is, what are all the different symbols that can be written on the two shared noticeboards?[2]

    Let n denotes the total number of tourists. In the deterministic solution, $n + 2$ different symbols are used. That is, one unique number is initially written on each one of the notepads, and each one of these n numbers can potentially be written on the noticeboards, plus 0 and "here."

---

[2]The two boards are implemented as two shared memory registers. The size of the registers to be allocated depends on the number of different symbols needed. So, the smaller the numbers of symbols used is the better.

Michael O. Rabin has proved that there is no deterministic solution using at most $\frac{1}{2}\sqrt[3]{n}$ symbols. Finding a tight bound is still an open problem.

As for the randomized solution, as was explained in Section 6.4, a fixed alphabet of $m + 2$ symbols suffice, for any number of tourists n, which achieves choice coordination with probability $1 - 1/2^{m/2}$. This implies that with $m + 2 = 256$, choice coordination will be achieved with probability $1 - 1/2^{127}$.

Thus, if we are willing to tolerate the practically negligible 2^{-127} probability of failure, then a fixed 256-symbol alphabet and a very simple algorithm will solve the problem independently of n. However, if we insist on probability 0 of failure and assume that initially the number that appears on the notepad of each tourist is unique, then the complexity goes up as $\frac{1}{2}\sqrt[3]{n}$ with the number n of tourists. So, to quote Michael O. Rabin, "perfectionism, it seems, does not pay!"

6.7 CHAPTER NOTES

The choice coordination problem was first introduced and solved by Michael O. Rabin in 1982. The results presented in this chapter are from Rabin's paper [41], except for the deterministic algorithm (page 45) which is new. The description of the problem as a group of tourists that should decide between two meeting places is by Annabelle McIver and Carroll Morgan [36]. The observation that mites employ an ear-choice coordination protocol involving chemical markings of trails, is based on the experiment reported by Asher E. Treat in [50]. Generalizations of the results for deciding between multiple alternatives are considered in [23].

The original deterministic algorithm presented in [41] is different and slightly more complicated than the algorithm presented in Section 6.5. For completeness, here is the description of the algorithm taken from [41]: "Informally the behavior of Pi, $1 \le i \le n$, is described as follows. When Pi first enters, if it sees 0 it prints i, and if it sees $1 \le j \le n$ it prints $\min(i, j)$; in either case Pi transfers sides. Later on, if m is the smallest non-zero integer in Pi's history and Pi currently sees $0 \le j \le n$, then Pi leaves $j < m$ unchanged and transfers, prints 0 and transfers if $m < j$, and prints e [i.e., "here"] if $j = m$. In short, Pi always 'becomes' Pm for the smallest $1 \le m \le n$ it has seen, replaces by 0 any $j > m$ it sees, and marks e when it sees its current name m for the second time."

Michael O. Rabin (born September 1, 1931) is an Israeli computer scientist who received the Turing Award in 1976 (with Dana S. Scott). "For their joint paper *Finite Automata and Their Decision Problem*, which introduced the idea of nondeterministic machines, which has proved to be an enormously valuable concept" [Extract from the Turing Award Citation]. The Turing Award is generally recognized as the highest distinction in computer science and the "Nobel Prize of Computing."

6.8   SELF REVIEW

Questions:

1. What would be the size of the alphabet needed, if we are willing to tolerate a 2^{-64} probability of failure?

2. Which of the two places will be chosen if:

    (a) All the tourists start the randomized algorithm at Notre-Dame de Paris cathedral?

    (b) All the tourists start the deterministic algorithm at Notre-Dame de Paris cathedral?

3. In the description of the deterministic algorithm, it is written: "Each tourist visits the two places *at most* three times after which the tourist goes inside one of them." Is it possible that some tourist will visit the two places exactly two times?

4. In the deterministic algorithm, how many times can the value on a noticeboard change not counting a change to "here?"

5. In the deterministic algorithm, can a tourist find in her/his second visit that $k = K$?

6. Find a deterministic solution for the case where a group of tourists has to decide between *three* meeting places for the beginning of a sightseeing tour: inside the Notre-Dame de Paris cathedral, inside the Louvre museum, or in the Luxembourg gardens. In fact, for any $k \geq 2$, find a deterministic solution for the case where a decision has to be made between k different meeting places.

7. Show that the case where a group of tourists has to decide between k meeting places is solvable by a deterministic algorithm if and only if the maximal number of tourists having the same initial number appearing on their notepads is smaller than the least prime divisor of k.

Answers:

1. A fixed 132-symbol alphabet is sufficient.

2. The Louvre museum in both cases.

3. Yes. This will happen when a tourist is the first to visit both locations.

4. At most once.

5. No.

6. We denote by v_i the initial *unique* number written on the notepad of *tourist*$_i$. Recall, that it is assumed that $v_i \neq 0$. *Tourist*$_i$ does the following: (1) on the first visit, if the value on the noticeboard equals 0, replace the 0 with v_i; (2) on later visits, write $v_i + 1$ on all the noticeboards with 0 value, if any exists; and (3) write "here" on the noticeboard with the minimum value.

7. See [23].

CHAPTER 7

Food for Thought

In distributed systems, concurrent access to *multiple* resources (like files, printers, memory locations, data structures) shared among several processors must be synchronized in order to avoid interference between conflicting operations. In particular, a well designed distributed system should never *deadlock*. The notion of a deadlock in the context of multiple resources is defined as follows,

> *A set of processors (or processes or computers) is deadlocked if each processor in the set is waiting for an event that only another processor in the set can cause.*

The event in the above definition is usually a release of a currently held resource, such as an exclusive permission to access a specific bank account. Thus, in a deadlock situation, there is a set of blocked processors each holding one or more resources and waiting to acquire a resource held by another processor in the set.

A simple example where a deadlock may occur is *bridge crossing*, where cars heading in the same direction can cross the bridge at the same time, but cars heading in opposite directions cannot. Thus, two cars coming from opposite direction can be stuck on the bridge if both try to cross the bridge at the same time. In this example, the resources are the two entrances to the bridge.

There are various approaches for finding when a system is deadlocked, and then resolving the deadlock situation. However, the best approach for handling deadlocks is to prevent them from ever happening. The dining philosophers problem is used to demonstrate how deadlocks can occur, and how they can be prevented.

7.1 THE DINING PHILOSOPHERS PROBLEM

The *dining philosophers* problem is a classical synchronization problem which models the allocation of resources in distributed systems.

A number of philosophers are seated around a table and half-way between each pair of adjacent philosophers there is a single fork (as illustrated in Figure 7.1). The life cycle of a philosopher consists of thinking, becoming hungry and trying to eat, eating, and then back to thinking, ad infinitum. Thus, a philosopher is at any time in one of the following three possible states: thinking, hungry, or eating.

A philosopher may transit from a thinking state to a hungry state spontaneously, at any time. To move from the hungry state to the eating state, a philosopher needs

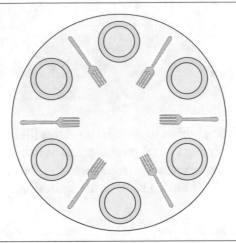

Figure 7.1: The dining philosophers problem. There is a fork between any two philosophers. A philosopher needs to get the two forks in order to eat.

to get the two forks close to him. Hence, neighboring philosophers cannot eat at the same time. It is assumed that eating times are finite. That is, a philosopher eats only for finite amount of time and after eating releases his two forks and resumes thinking.

The problem is to design a strategy (i.e., an algorithm) for each one of the philosophers which will never deadlock. That is, to decide in which order a philosopher has to *acquire*, *wait for* and *release* forks to prevent a deadlock from ever happening.[1]

Freedom from deadlock (or deadlock-freedom) means that if at any time there is a hungry philosopher then at a later time some philosopher will eat. Most of the solutions will enjoy a stronger property, called freedom from starvation (or starvation-freedom), in which each hungry philosopher eventually gets to eat.

Early algorithms made use of some centralized mechanism, allowing only one philosopher to eat at any instant. However, it seems more reasonable to require an algorithm to be concurrent; that is, philosophers interact only with nearby philosophers when acquiring forks. A concurrent algorithm decreases the likelihood that an action of one philosopher will affect other distant philosophers.

The control of each fork is *isolated* from the other forks: the philosophers may acquire and release forks only one at a time. We avoid referring to the specific details of the implementation of how a single fork is acquired, and only assume that the implementation is *fair* in the following

---

[1]Buying more forks is not an option :)

senses: a process cannot acquire and release a specific fork infinitely often, while some other process that is continuously waiting to acquire this fork, never gets a chance to do so.

7.2   APPLICATIONS

To see the corresponding synchronization problem for computing systems, think of the philosophers as processors (or computers). The forks correspond to the various resources (for example, exclusive access to a bank account) a processor may need to acquire in order to be able to complete a certain operation. For example, to transfer money between two accounts, the processor must lock (i.e., get exclusive access to) both accounts to ensure the correct value is debited from one account and credited to another.

Continuing with the money transfer example, the dining philosopher example is somewhat oversimplified, by having each account (fork) accessible by only two clerks (philosophers). So, how can deadlock be prevented assuming that there are thousands of clerks and millions of bank accounts, and each clerk may access each of the accounts? There is a very simple practical technique, called the total order technique which is described in the next section, which prevents deadlocks from ever happening even in such complex situations.

In any case, the primary purpose of the dining philosophers problem is to give a clean, abstract, even simplified specification for processor interactions that can be used as teaching examples. In particular, to demonstrate how a deadlock can occur and how it can be prevented.

7.3   DEADLOCK PREVENTION: THE TOTAL ORDER TECHNIQUE

A well-known deadlock prevention technique, called the total order technique, is to impose a total ordering of all the resources, and to require that each processor requests the resources in an increasing order. More precisely:

> Assume that all the resources are numbered and that there is a total order between the numbers of the different resources.[2] If each processor requests resources in an increasing order of enumeration, then deadlock is not possible.

The total order technique guarantees that there is no cycle involving several processors, where each is waiting for a resource held by the next one in the cycle. Thus, deadlock is not possible. When using the total order technique, if a needed resource is not available, the processor waits until the resource becomes available, without releasing any of the resources it has already managed to lock. This type of techniques is called *hold and wait*.

This simple technique, where each processor requests resources in an increasing order of enumeration, can now be used to solve the problem of transferring money between two bank

---

[2]There is a total order among the numbers of the different resources, if for any two resources, it is always the case that the number of one of them is strictly bigger than the other.

accounts. There is a total order between account numbers. The account numbers are used as the resource numbers, and the locking of the two accounts is done in an increasing order. The total order technique guarantees that this solution is indeed without a deadlock.

The technique can also be used to solve the dining philosophers problem as follows. First the forks are numbered consecutively around the table from 1 to n, where n is the number of forks. Once all the forks are numbered, each philosopher always acquires the two forks in an increasing order of enumeration. Notice that once each philosopher knows which fork, the left one or the right one, he should try to acquire first, there is no need to "remember" the numbering of the forks.

This simple solution has a major drawback: it is possible to get into a situation in which all the philosophers are hungry, and only one of them can eat while all the others have to wait for him to finish eating and release the forks. Below we present a few solutions that are more efficient.

7.4   HOLD AND WAIT STRATEGY: THE LR ALGORITHM

We first present an algorithm in which a hungry philosopher acquires his forks in some specified order. If a fork is not available when requested, the philosopher waits until the fork is released by his neighbor and then takes it. If the philosopher acquires one fork and the other fork is not immediately available, he holds the acquired fork until the other fork is released.

According to this strategy, each philosopher is either an *L-type* philosopher which means that a philosopher first obtains his left fork and then his right fork, or an *R-type* philosopher which means that a philosopher first obtains his right fork and then his left fork.

We observe that a strategy where every hungry philosopher first tries to obtain his left fork and then his right fork (i.e., all the philosophers are L-type) *can* deadlock. To see that, assume that all the philosophers become hungry at the same time. Each one of them succeeds in obtaining his left fork and then waits forever for his right fork to be released by his neighbor to the right.

We will assume that the philosophers are numbered consecutively around the table from 1 to n, where n is the number of philosophers. This numbering is used only to assign a strategy to each philosopher.

The LR algorithm: The philosophers are assigned fork acquisition strategies as follows: the philosophers whose numbers are even are R-type, and the philosophers whose numbers are odd are L-type.

Next, we show that the LR algorithm is deadlock-free. For proving that claim, we make use of the total order technique. Recall that, according to this technique, when all the resources are numbered, deadlock is not possible if each processor acquires resources in an increasing order of enumeration.

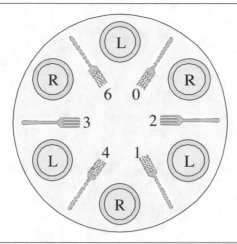

Figure 7.2: The LR algorithm. With respect to the numbering of the forks, the algorithm where each philosopher tries to lock its two forks in an increasing order of enumeration is the LR algorithm.

We start the proof by numbering all the forks as follows. We pick an arbitrary fork and number it 0. Let f be a fork at distance i (counting clockwise) from the 0 fork. If i is even then we number f with the number $i - 1$, otherwise, we number f with the number $i + 1$. For six philosophers, the resulting numbering of the forks would be 0, 2, 1, 4, 3, 6. The resulting numbering is illustrated in Figure 7.2. With respect to this numbering, the algorithm where each philosopher tries to lock his two forks in an increasing order of enumeration is *exactly* the LR algorithm. Hence, according to the total order technique, the LR algorithm is deadlock-free.

Concurrency in the context of the dining philosophers problem is a measure of how many philosophers can eat simultaneously (in the worst case) when all the philosophers are hungry. Having high concurrency is a most desirable property. The LR algorithm does not achieve high concurrency: it is possible to get into a situation in which only a *quarter* of the philosophers will be able to eat simultaneously when all of them are hungry. (Such a situation is described in Section 7.9.)

7.5   HOLD AND WAIT STRATEGY: THE LLR ALGORITHM

The following algorithm, called the LLR algorithm is better than the LR algorithm in terms of concurrency. It guarantees that at least a *third* of the philosophers will always be able to eat simultaneously when all of them are hungry. Recall that the philosophers are numbered consecutively around the table from 1 to n.

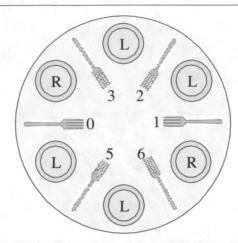

Figure 7.3: The LLR algorithm. With respect to this numbering, the algorithm where each philosopher tries to lock its two forks in an increasing order of enumeration is exactly the LLR algorithm.

> *The LLR algorithm*: The philosophers are assigned fork acquisition strategies as follows: philosopher i is R-type if i is divisible by 3, L-type otherwise.

We show that the LLR algorithm is deadlock-free. For proving that claim we again make use of the total order technique.

We start by numbering all the forks as follows. We pick an arbitrary fork and number it 0. Let f be a fork at distance i (counting clockwise) from the 0 fork. If $(i \bmod 3) = 1$ then we number f with the number $i + 2$; if $(i \bmod 3) = 2$ then we number f with the number i; if $(i \bmod 3) = 0$ then we number f with the number $i - 2$. Notice that there is a total order between the numbers of the different forks, that is, no two forks get the same number. For six philosophers, the resulting numbering of the forks would be 0, 3, 2, 1, 6, 5. The resulting numbering is illustrated in Figure 7.3. With respect to this numbering, the algorithm where each philosopher tries to lock its two forks in an increasing order of enumeration is exactly the LLR algorithm. Hence, according to the total order technique, the algorithm is deadlock-free.

7.6 WAIT AND RELEASE STRATEGY: THE WAIT/RELEASE ALGORITHM

We now consider algorithms in which a philosopher may release a held fork before eating. In particular, if a philosopher obtains one fork, and the other fork is not free, the held fork is released and the philosopher starts over. Recall that we assume that the philosophers are ordered around the table from 1 to n.

The wait/release algorithm: A philosopher whose number is odd first waits until his left fork is free, and then takes it. If his right fork is free, he takes it and then eats. Otherwise, he releases his left fork and begins again. A philosopher whose number is even first waits until his right fork is free, and then takes it. If his left fork is free, he takes it and then eats. Otherwise, he releases his right fork and begins again.

The algorithm is free from deadlocks and guarantees that at least a *third* of the philosophers will be able to eat simultaneously when all of them are hungry. The proof that the algorithm is deadlock-free, follows from the observation that every starved philosopher, except may one (when their number is odd), must have a neighbor who does not starve.

Unlike any algorithm constructed according to the hold and wait strategy, the wait/release algorithm satisfies the following *robustness* property: for an even number of philosophers, if all the philosophers except for three consecutive philosophers die (even while eating), then one of the three philosophers will always be able to eat when he becomes hungry. It has been shown that no hold and wait algorithm satisfies such a robustness property. Thus, the wait and release strategy can attain a level of robustness that the hold and wait strategy cannot.

7.7   WAIT AND RELEASE STRATEGY: A RANDOMIZED ALGORITHM

A *randomized* algorithm is an algorithm that in the course of its action can toss a coin, and uses its outcome to decide what to do next. An algorithm which is not randomized is called a *deterministic* algorithm. In the context of the dining philosophers problem, in a randomized algorithm, a philosopher can use coin tossing and uses its outcome to decide what to do next.

A *symmetric* algorithm is an algorithm where the strategies for all philosophers are identical. There is a simple argument which proves that there does not exist a symmetric deterministic algorithm for the dining philosophers problem which is deadlock-free. In particular, the algorithms shown earlier do not satisfy this constraint; in those algorithms, the actions carried out by a philosopher depend on the philosopher's position in a global ordering around the table. However, there does exist a symmetric randomized algorithm which is deadlock-free. In such an algorithm, randomization is used to break symmetry.

In practice, using symmetric algorithms significantly simplifies the design of concurrent systems. The advantage of using symmetric algorithms is that all the processors follow the same strategy, and hence there is no need to assign different strategies based on a global ordering. As a result, new processors can easily be added or removed from the system without affecting the other processors.

We now present a symmetric randomized algorithm: each philosopher begins the algorithm in the same state, and the code for all the philosophers is identical. In addition to using randomization, we also apply the wait and release strategy.

THE FREE PHILOSOPHERS ALGORITHM: Code for a philosopher

$R(\cdot)$ is the reflection function on *{right,left}*

```
1  repeat forever
2      think
3      become hungry
4      repeat
5          s ← a random element from {right,left}
6          await (s fork is free) and then take it
7          if R(s) fork is free then take R(s) else release s fork fi
8      until (holding both forks)
9      eat
10     release both forks
11 end
```

Figure 7.4: The code of the free philosophers algorithm.

The free philosophers algorithm: a philosopher first flips a fair coin and according to the outcome, decides whether he should first try to obtain his left fork or his right fork.

If the outcome is "heads," the philosopher first waits until his left fork is free, and then takes it. If his right fork is free, he takes it and then eats. Otherwise, he releases his left fork and starts over by flipping the coin again.

If the outcome is "tails," the philosopher first waits until his right fork is free, and then takes it. If his left fork is free, he takes it and then eats. Otherwise, he releases his right fork and starts over by flipping the coin again.

The free philosophers algorithm is deadlock-free.[3] Moreover, the algorithm satisfies the same robustness property as the algorithm on page 56, constructed according to the wait and release strategy. That is, if all the philosophers except for three consecutive philosophers die (even while eating), then one of the three philosophers will always be able to eat when he becomes hungry.

The code is given in Figure 7.4. It can be skipped without loss of continuity. For two values x and y, R is the reflection function on $\{x, y\}$ if $x = R(y)$ and $y = R(x)$.

---

[3]Actually, we mean that the randomized algorithm is deadlock-free *with probability* 1. Intuitively, this means that in the course of an infinite time period, the chances of a deadlock occurring are zero.

7.8   CHAPTER NOTES

In 1968, Edsger Wybe Dijkstra identified the problem of preventing and avoiding deadlocks and described it as follows: "This situation, when one process can continue only provided the other one is killed first, is called *the deadly embrace*. The problem to be solved is: how can we avoid the danger of the deadly embrace without being unnecessarily restrictive" [14].

There are several simple design principles which, when applied properly, prevent the occurrence of deadlocks, such as the (hold and wait) total order technique. Two other known (wait and release) techniques are two-phase locking [17] and timestamping ordering [6].

The dining philosophers problem was introduced by Edsger W. Dijkstra in 1971 [15]. The LR algorithm (page 54) seems to be folklore and has appeared in various papers [9, 10]. The LLR algorithm (page 55) was proposed by S. P. Rana and D. K. Banerji in [43], where it is also shown that the LLR algorithm is better than the LR algorithm in terms of concurrency. Exact proofs regarding concurrency and robustness of the algorithms, as well as a proof that the wait and release strategy can attain a level of robustness that the hold and wait strategy cannot, can be found in [48].

The Free Philosophers Algorithm was suggested by Daniel Lehmann and Michael O. Rabin in [34]. Randomized algorithms were introduced in the seventies by Michael O. Rabin [42], and since then had a tremendous impact on the design of algorithms in all areas of computer science.

The drinking philosophers which generalize the dining philosophers problem is introduced in [11]. In [4], a few algorithms for the dining/drinking philosophers problem are presented in various models.

7.9   SELF REVIEW

Questions:

1. Consider a (hold and wait) algorithm where exactly one philosopher is an R-type and each one of the others is an L-type. Show that it is possible to get into a situation in which all the philosophers are hungry, and only one of them can eat while all the others have to wait for him to finish eating and release the forks.

2. Is it true that deadlock is not possible in any (hold and wait) algorithm where (1) each philosopher is either an L-type or an R-type, (2) at least one philosopher is an L-type, and (3) at least one philosopher is an R-type?

3. In Section 7.6 (page 56), it is claimed that the fact that the wait/release algorithm is deadlock-free, follows from the observation that every starved philosopher, except may one, must have a neighbor who does not starve. Explain why this observation is valid.

4. Recall that the freedom from starvation property means that each hungry philosopher eventually gets to eat. Are the LR, the LLR, and the wait/release algorithms starvation-free?

5. On page 55 it is claimed that: "The LR algorithm does not achieve high concurrency: it is possible to get into a situation in which only a *quarter* of the philosophers will be able to eat simultaneously when all of them are hungry." Explain why this claim is valid.

6. On page 55 it is claimed that: the LLR algorithm "guarantees that at least a *third* of the philosophers will always be able to eat simultaneously when all of them are hungry." Explain why this claim is valid.

Answers:

1. Assume all the philosophers are hungry. Let each L-type philosopher pick his left fork. There is one free fork left. Let the L-type philosopher who is close to this free fork pick it up and eat. No other philosopher can acquire two forks and eat at this configuration.

2. Yes. There is a simple proof which is based on the total order technique.

3. Assume for simplicity that the number of philosophers is even. An $\mathcal{L}$-*type* philosopher is a philosopher that first waits until its left fork is free, and an $\mathcal{R}$-*type* philosopher is a philosopher that first waits until its right fork is free. Suppose without loss of generality that an $\mathcal{L}$-type philosopher p is starved. By the assumption (from page 52) that the allocation of a single fork is fair, p will acquire its left fork infinitely often. This means that, since he is starved, his right fork is always in use when he tries to take it. However, since his right neighbor p' is $\mathcal{R}$-type, p' must be holding both forks whenever p tries to take the fork between them. Since p fails to obtain his forks infinitely often, p' must eat infinitely often; in other words, every starved philosopher has a neighbor who does not starve.

4. The LR the LLR algorithms are starvation-free, the wait/release algorithm is not. To see that the wait/release algorithm is not starvation-free consider a system with two philosophers, named Alice and Bob. Alice first waits until her left fork is free and Bob first waits until his right fork is free. The two forks are named f_1 and f_2. Whenever Alice wants to eat she tries to pick up f_1 first. We consider a scenario in which Alice eats infinitely often, and thus she holds f_1 infinitely often. Now, we arrange that whenever Bob tries to acquire f_1 (while holding f_2) he finds that f_1 is held by Alice. Thus, Bob never gets to eat.

5. We assume for simplicity that the number of philosophers, n, is divisible by 4. That is, $n \equiv 0 \bmod 4$. Consider the following scenario.

   (a) Each R-type philosopher i, where $i \equiv 0 \bmod 4$, becomes hungry, picks up both forks and eats.

(b) Each L-type philosopher i, where $i \equiv (0 \bmod 4) + 1$, becomes hungry and waits for its left fork to be released.

(c) Each L-type philosopher i, where $i \equiv (0 \bmod 4) + 3$, becomes hungry, picks up its left fork, and then waits for its right fork to be released.

(d) Each R-type philosopher i, where $i \equiv (0 \bmod 4) + 2$, becomes hungry and waits for its right fork to be released.

Clearly, in this scenario, at most $n/4$ philosophers can eat simultaneously.

6. We call a sequence of 3 consecutive philosophers a 3-chain and refer to the philosophers in this chain as $p_1 p_2 p_3$. The fork to the right of p_i will be called f_i; fork f_i is shared by p_i and p_{i+1}. A 3-chain LLR of philosophers is a 3-chain where the first and second philosophers are L-type and the third philosopher is an R-type. We show that when all the philosophers want to eat, in the 3-chain LLR at least one of the three philosophers can eat. Since the 3-chain LLR repeats $\lfloor n/3 \rfloor$ times, the result will follow.

Consider the 3-chain LLR of philosophers p_1, p_2, and p_3. If p_1 acquires both forks, the proof is completed. So, assume that p_1 is waiting for a fork. There are two possible cases: (1) p_1 is waiting for f_0 (its left fork); or (2) p_1 is waiting for f_1 (its right fork).

Case 1: In this case, p_2 can always get f_1 and then compete for f_2. If p_3 is not competing for f_2 then p_2 will get f_2, and we are done. However, if p_3 is also competing for f_2, then both p_2 and p_3 are competing for their second fork, and the one to succeed in this competition will have both forks and will be able to eat.

Case 2: In this case, p_1 already holds f_0 and is waiting for f_1. If p_2 is not competing, then p_1 will get its second fork, and we are done. So let's assume that p_2 is competing and succeeds in getting f_1. We now continue as in case 1. If p_3 is not competing for f_2 then p_2 will get f_2, and we are done. However, if p_3 is also competing for f_2, then both p_2 and p_3 are competing for their second fork, and the one to succeed in this competition will have both forks and will be able to eat.

CHAPTER 8

All for One and One for All

Our story begins with ten kids that were recently invited to play at the playground at the queen's palace. These ten kids (five boys and five girls) are known to be the smartest kids in the kingdom, and the queen has invited them so that she can test whether they are as smart as claimed.

8.1 THE SEE-SAW PUZZLE

The playground resides in the center of a beautiful garden, and it has two see-saws in it: a black colored see-saw and a white colored see-saw. Each see-saw has a left side and a right side, and its two possible positions are called "left side down" and "right side down," which indicate which side is down (implying that the opposite side is up). The queen has told the kids that they will be able to get whatever they want if they could solve her challenge. She has described the challenge as follows.

"Whenever I feel like it, I will select one kid and lead him or her to the playground. At the playground, the kid will be allowed to change the position of each one of the see-saws (either from 'left-side-down' to 'right-side-down' or vice versa), or the kid may leave them unchanged. Nobody except the kids will ever change the position of the sea-saws."

Afterward, the kid will be led back to the palace, and I will continue selecting kids and lead them to the playground. Some kids may be selected more often than others. Each kid will visit the playground arbitrarily often.

When you think that all of you have visited the playground at least once, one of you should announce that this has happened. If you are correct, you will be able to ask for whatever you want, and it will be given to you. If you are wrong, you will get nothing!

You will have one chance now to confer with each other and devise a plan. In your plan you should take into consideration the following two facts.

1. You will not know which position the see-saws are in to begin with.

2. The plan should be such that all of you will follow exactly the same rules, in particular, you are not allowed to designate one kid as a leader who will behave differently than others.

After that, you will be kept in separate rooms in the palace and have no chance at further verbal communication."

The kids have devised the following plan to resolve the queen's challenge using only the see-saws to communicate. Using their plan they will be able to say with absolute certainty that each kid has visited the playground at least one. What is the plan?

8.2   APPLICATIONS

The see-saw puzzle is a coordination problem. Solving it amounts to solving a classical synchronization problem for computers, called *barrier synchronization*, using only two shared bits. (A bit is a location in memory that at any time can hold one of two values, 0 or 1.) Before we show how to solve the see-saw puzzle, we explain what barrier synchronization is all about.

It is sometimes convenient to write concurrent computer programs that are divided into phases such that no processor may proceed into the next phase until all processors have finished the current phase and are ready to move into the next phase together. In such programs, each phase typically depends on the results of the previous phase. For example, all the processors may participate in solving problem #1, and no processor is allowed to start solving problem #2 before all other processors are done with problem #1. This type of a behavior can be achieved by placing a *barrier* at the end of each phase, which ensures that all processors have reached a certain point in a computation before any of them can proceed.[2]

More precisely, a barrier is a coordination mechanism that forces processors (or computers) which participate in a joint activity to wait until each one of them has reached a certain point in its program. The collection of these coordination points is called the barrier. Once all the processors have reached the barrier, they are all permitted to continue past the barrier.

Using barriers enables us, in various cases, to significantly simplify the task of designing concurrent programs. The programmer may write the program under the assumption that it should work correctly only when it executes in a *synchronous* environment, where the processors run at the same speed. Then, by using barriers for synchronization, the program can be adapted to work also in an *asynchronous* environment, where no assumption is made about the relative speed of the processors. Such an approach is, in particular, helpful for the design of numerical and scientific algorithms.

Going back to the see-saw puzzle, a kid that enters the playground corresponds to a processor that has reached the barrier, the kids' plan is the barrier's coordination mechanism, and announcing that all the kids have visited the playground corresponds to the fact that all the processors have reached the barrier, and that they are all permitted to continue past the barrier.

---

[1]This should explain the title of this chapter.

A SOLUTION FOR THE SEE-SAW PUZZLE FOR TEN KIDS: FIRST PLAN

local variables:

leader: boolean, initial value of exactly one kid is *true* and all others are *false*

local.counter: integer, initial value is 0

Assumptions:

The initial value of leader variable of exactly one kid is *true*

The see-saw is in the "left-side-down" position to begin with

Each time a kid enters the playground the kid does the following:

```
1  if leader = true then                                    // I'm the leader
2      if see-saw = left-side-down then see-saw ←right-side-down
3      else {see-saw ←left-side-down; counter ← counter + 1
5          if counter = 9 then announce that all the kids have visited the playground}
4  else                                                      // I'm not the leader
5      if counter = 0 then
6          if see-saw = left-side-down then {see-saw ←right-side-down; counter ← 1}
```

Figure 8.1: The kids' first plan.

8.3 THE KIDS' FIRST PLAN

The kids decided to solve the problem in several steps. First, they have devised the following plan assuming that they do know which position the see-saws are in, to begin with, and that they do not all have to follow the same rules. In this plan, there is a need to use only the *black* colored see-saw. The kids have assumed that the initial position of the (black) see-saw is "left-side-down."

The kids have designated one kid as a leader whose responsibility is to count how many kids have visited the playground at least once and to be the one to announce that all the 10 kids have visited the playground. The leader counter is initially set to 0. Since the kids cannot communicate verbally, the only way for them to communicate is by changing the position of the see-saw according to the following strategy.

When the leader enters the playground he does as follows: If the see-saw position is "right-side-down," he changes the position to "left-side-down," and increments his count by one. When the count reaches 9, he announces that all the 10 kids have visited the playground. If the see-saw position is "left-side-down" (i.e., the initial position), he does nothing.

A SOLUTION FOR THE SEE-SAW PUZZLE FOR TEN KIDS: SECOND PLAN

local variables:

leader: boolean, initial value of exactly one kid is *true* and all others are *false*

local.counter: integer, initial value is 0

Assumptions:

The initial value of leader variable of exactly one kid is *true*

The initial position of the see-saw is not a priori known

Each time a kid enters the playground the kid does the following:

```
1 if leader = true then                                    // I'm the leader
2      if see-saw = left-side-down then see-saw ←right-side-down
3      else {see-saw ←left-side-down; counter ← counter + 1
5          if counter = 18 then announce that all the kids have visited the playground}
4 else                                                     // I'm not the leader
5      if counter < 2 then
6          if see-saw = left-side-down
7          then {see-saw ←right-side-down; counter ← counter + 1}
```

Figure 8.2: The kids' second plan.

When any other kid enters the playground he or she does as follows. The first time she finds that the see-saw position is "left-side-down" (i.e., the initial position) she changes the position to "right-side-down." Otherwise, she does nothing.

We notice that only the leader will ever set the see-saw back to the "left-side-down" position and that any other kid changes the position exactly once to "right-side-down" to signal to the leader that he or she has been there. The code is given in Figure 8.1. This and the other code segments in this chapter can be skipped without loss of continuity.

8.4 THE KIDS' SECOND PLAN

After the kids have devised this plan, they considered how to modify it, to cover the case where the initial position of the see-saw is not known. The reason why they cannot use their previous plan is that the see-saw may be in the "right-side-down" position to begin with. If the leader sees this, he would erroneously count this as +1 and could announce they have all visited the playground too early. Unfortunately, the leader cannot just wait until he counts one more (10 in this case), as he may wait forever when the see-saw is in the "left-side-down" position to begin with.

To resolve this problem, the kids have decided to have each kid signal her presence in the playground *twice* and have the leader wait until he counts up to 18. Then they can be certain every kid has visited the playground at least once. More precisely, their new plan is as follows.

As before the kids have designated one kid as a leader, whose initial count is 0.

When the leader enters the playground he does as follows: If the see-saw position is "right-side-down," he changes the position to "left-side-down," and increments his count by one. When the count reaches 18, he announces that all the 10 kids have visited the playground. If the see-saw position is "left-side-down" (i.e., the initial position) he does nothing.

When any other kid enters the playground he or she does as follows: The first *two* times she finds that the see-saw position is "left-side-down" (i.e., the initial position) she changes the position to "right-side-down." Otherwise, she does nothing.

The code is given in Figure 8.2. Finding these solutions is relatively easy. But the queen has explicitly said that the kids are not allowed to choose a leader! And that the initial position of the see-saw is not known. Resolving this issue is hard. It is not enough to simply modify the previous plan. A completely new strategy is needed which will make use of both the black and the white see-saws. Below we describe the final plan the kids have devised to solve the queen's challenge.

8.5   THE KIDS' FINAL PLAN

According to the plan the kids will play in the playground, adhering to strict rules. All the kids will play according to the same set of rules. At any moment, either the left side or the right side of each see-saw is up.

When each kid first enters the playground, he or she sits on the side which is currently the up-side of the *black* see-saw causing it to swing to the ground (and hence to become the down-side). Once a kid exits the playground (giving another kid a chance to enter it), it would be convenient to imagine the kid is still setting on one side of the see-saw (although physically he is not there anymore). Thus, although physically at any given time there is at most one kid in the playground, we would imagine there may be several kids sitting on the see-saw at the same time.

Each kid remembers whether he sits on the left side or the right side of the black see-saw. Only a kid who is currently sitting on the ground (i.e., on the side which is currently the down-side) can get off and when he does the see-saw must swing to the opposite orientation. Once a kid gets off, by applying the proper rule, we may no longer imagine that he is still on the see-saw. These rules enforce a balance invariant which says that the number of kids on each side of the see-saw differs by at most one. We notice that by the above description of how a kid gets on and off the see-saw: (1) when the number of kids on each side of the see-saw is the same, the side which was initially the down-side is currently the up-side; and (2) when the number of kids on each side of the see-saw differs by one, the side which was initially the down-side is heavier and is currently the down-side (the heavier side is always the down-side).

Each kid enters the playground with two tokens. The plan will force the kids on the bottom of the black see-saw to give away tokens to the kids on the top of the see-saw. Thus, the token flow will change direction depending on the orientation of the see-saw. Tokens can be neither created nor destroyed. The idea of the plan devised by the kids is to cause tokens to concentrate in the hands of a single kid. Hence, eventually some kid will see at least 20 tokens, and this kid will announce that all kids have visited the playground.

Following is the complete description of the plan. From now on, whenever we refer to a see-saw without mentioning a specific color, we will mean the black see-saw. Also, we will call the white see-saw the *token slot*, and will call its two possible states "token present" and "no token present." The token slot either contains a token or is empty, according to its current state. Recall that the black see-saw has a left side and a right side and that its two states are called "left side down" and "right side down," which indicate which side is down (implying that the opposite side is up).

Each kid always remembers the number of tokens it currently possesses and which of four states it is currently in with respect to the see-saw: "never been on," "on left side," "on right side," and "got off." A kid is said to be on the up-side of the see-saw if the kid is currently "on left side" and the see-saw is in state "right side down," or it is currently "on right side" and the see-saw is in state "left side down." Every kid initially possesses *two* tokens and is in state "never been on."

We define the plan by a list of rules. When a kid enters the playground, the kid looks at the see-saws and at his internal state and carries out the first applicable rule, if any. If no rule is applicable, the kid does nothing which leaves his internal state and the states of the see-saws unchanged.

Rule 1: (Start) *Applicable if the kid in the playground is in state "never been on." The kid gets on the up-side of the see-saw and changes the current state of the see-saw. By "get on," we mean that the kid changes his (or her) internal state to "on left side" or "on right side" according to whichever side is up. Since changing the state of the see-saw causes that side to go down, the kid ends up on the down-side of the see-saw.*

Rule 2: (Emitter) *Applicable if the kid in the playground is on the down-side of the see-saw, has one or more tokens, and the token slot is empty. The kid flips (the position of) the token slot (to indicate that a token is present) and decrements by one the count of tokens he possesses. If his token count thereby becomes zero, the kid gets off the see-saw by setting his state to "got off" and flips the position of the see-saw.*

Rule 3: (Absorber) *Applicable if the kid in the playground is on the up-side of the see-saw and a token is present in the token slot. The kid flips the position of the token slot (to indicate that a token is no longer present) and increments by one the count of tokens he possesses.*

Rule 4: (End of game) *Applicable if the kid in the playground is on the see-saw and sees at least 20 tokens, where the number of tokens the kid sees is the number she possesses, plus one if a token is present in the token slot. The kid thus knows that all the 10 kids have visited the playground at least once, and announces that fact.*

This completes the description of the kids' final plan. The code of the plan is given in Figure 8.3. For two values x and y, R is the reflection function on $\{x, y\}$ if $x = R(y)$ and $y = R(x)$.

8.6   FURTHER EXPLANATIONS

We prove below that the kids' plan indeed solves the queen's challenge. The two main ideas behind the kids' final plan can be stated as the following two invariants.

> **Token invariant:** *The number of tokens is either 20 or 21 and does not change at any time. (The number of tokens is the total number of tokens possessed by all of the kids, plus 1 if a token is present in the token slot.)*

To see why the token invariant holds, notice that the number of tokens in the starting configuration is 20 with the possible addition of one token present in the token slot. The rules that effect tokens are rules 2 and 3 both of which maintain the token invariant.

> **Balance invariant:** *The number of kids on the left and right sides of the see-saw is either perfectly balanced or favors the down-side of the see-saw by one kid.*

To see why the token invariant holds, notice that the see-saw starts empty, zero on either side. Rule 1 preserves the invariant because a kid gets on the up side and then flips the see-saw. If a kid runs out of tokens, it must be on the down side of the see-saw; hence, when rule 2 is applied the invariant is maintained.

Using the token invariant and the balance invariant, we can now justify the correctness of the kids' plan. By the token invariant, there are no more than $2n + 1$ tokens in the system. At most two come from each player; at most one comes from the initialized state of the token slot. Hence, if a kid sees $2k$ tokens, it has to be the case that at least k kids have visited the playground at least once.

Next, we argue that eventually there will be a time where everybody has visited the playground and there is exactly one kid that sees 20 tokens. We know there will be a time when everybody has visited the playground. Furthermore, for any number of kids, say m kids ($m > 2$), still active on the see-saw, there will be a future time when there are only $m - 1$ kids on the see-saw: by the balance invariant, there are some kids on both sides and hence eventually either rule 2 or rule 3 is applicable (i.e., there is no deadlock). Each kid has visited the playground, hence, rule 1 will no longer apply. Applying rules 2 and 3 will cause tokens to flow from the down side to the up side; eventually the token count of a down side kid will become zero and the kid will get off the see-saw. Hence, eventually there will be exactly one kid that will see

---

A SOLUTION FOR THE SEE-SAW PUZZLE FOR n KIDS: THE FINAL PLAN

type   *token.states* = ranges over {token-present, no-token-present}

         see-saw.states = ranges over {left-side-down, right-side-down}

shared *token*: a bit ranges over *token.states*

         see-saw: a bit ranges over *see-saw.states*

local   *mystate*: 4-valued register, ranges over {never-been-on, on-left-side, on-right-side, got-off},

         initial value "never-been-on"   // never-been-on

         mytokens: register, ranges over {0, ..., $2n+1$}, initial value is 2   // two tokens

$R(\cdot)$ is the reflection function on {left-side-down, right-side-down}

Each time a kid enters the playground the kid does the following:

1 **if** *mystate* = never-been-on **then**   // **Rule 1: Start**

2   **if** *see-saw* = left-side-down **then** *mystate* ← on-right-side // gets on up-side

3   **else** *mystate* ← on-left-side

4   *see-saw* ← R(*see-saw*)   // flips the see-saw bit

                                          // **Rule 2: Emitter**

5 **elseif** *token* = no-token-present **and**   // token bit empty?

6   ((*mystate* = on-left-side **and** *see-saw* = left-side-down) **or**   // on the

7   (*mystate* = on-right-side **and** *see-saw* = right-side-down)) **then**   // down-side?

8   *token* ← token-present   // emit a token

9   *mytokens* ← *mytokens* − 1   // one token less

10   **if** *mytokens* = 0 **then**   // no more tokens?

11   *mystate* ← got-off   // gets off the see-saw

12   *see-saw* ← R(*see-saw*)   // flips the see-saw bit

                                          // **Rule 3: Absorber**

13 **elseif** *token* = token-present **and**   // token bit full?

14   ((*mystate* = on-left-side **and** *see-saw* = right-side-down) **or**   // on the

15   (*mystate* = on-right-side **and** *see-saw* = left-side-down)) **then**   // up-side?

16   *token* ← no-token-present   // absorb a token

17   *mytokens* ← *mytokens* + 1   // one token more

                                        // **Rule 4: End of game**

18 **elseif** *mytokens* $\geq 2n$ **or**   // all n processes

19   (*mytokens* = $2n - 1$ **and** *token* = token-present) **then**   // have arrived?

20   announce that all the kids have visited the playground   // notifies all

---

Figure 8.3: The kids' final plan. The shared see-saw bit and token bit can be inspected and modified together in one atomic step, and their initial values are not *a priori* known.

20 tokens and will know that all other kids visited the playground. When this happens, this kid will correctly announce that all kids have visited the playground. This completes the correctness proof.

8.7   CHAPTER NOTES

The queen has promised the kids that if they solve her challenge, each one of them will be able to ask for whatever he or she wants and that all the kids' requests will be fulfilled. Now that you know that the kids have passed the queen's test, what would you advise them to ask for?

The final plan of the kids as described here was published by Michael J. Fischer, Shlomo Moran, Steven Rudich, and Gadi Taubenfeld in [21]. In practice, implementations of the kids' first and second plans are used for solving the barrier synchronization problem.

The first paper on the topic of barrier synchronization is by Harry Jordan [29]. There are dozens of important papers about barrier synchronization. Section 5 of [48] gives detailed coverage of the topic.

"All for one and one for all, united we stand divided we fall," is the motto of the title characters in the book *The Three Musketeers*, by the 19th-century French author Alexandre Dumas [16].

8.8   SELF REVIEW

Questions:

1. Show that the kids' final plan can easily be adapted to work for any number of kids, not just ten kids.

2. It is assumed that each kid initially possesses *two* tokens. Why is one token not enough?

3. In the kids' final plan, is it possible that when one kid announces that all the kids have visited the playground, there is another kid who is still on the see-saw?

Answers:

1. Let n denotes the number of kids. Then, in Rule 4 replace the number 20 with $2n$.

2. Given that the token slot can initially be empty or full, when a kid sees ten tokens, he or she cannot know for sure that all the kids have visited the playground. On the other hand, a kid cannot wait for 11 tokens as he or she may wait forever in case the token slot was initially empty.

3. Yes.

CHAPTER 9

The World is a Playground

Recall our story from Chapter 8. Ten bright kids were invited by the queen to play at the playground. The playground resides in the center of a beautiful garden at the queen's palace, and it has two see-saws in it which, in this chapter, will be named see-saw #1 and see-saw #2. Each see-saw has a left side and a right side, and its two possible positions are called "left-side-down" and "right-side-down," which indicate which side is down (implying that the opposite side is up).

After the kids have solved the see-saw puzzle (from Chapter 8), they were very excited and asked the queen to rechallenge them. The queen told them that since they have to return home soon, she will ask them an easier (but not easy) question.

9.1   THE GREEN-OR-BLUE GAME

The queen described her challenge as follows.

> "Only two of you, Adam and Eve, will participate in the game. Whenever I feel like it, I will select Eve or Adam and lead her or him to the playground. At the playground the kid will be allowed to check the position of *only one* see-saw and then may change the position of that see-saw (either from "left-side-down" to "right-side-down" or vice versa), or the kid may leave the see-saw unchanged. The kid will not be able to check the position of both see-saws and then change one of them, nor will the kid be able to check the position of one see-saw and then change the position of the other see-saw.
>
> Before a kid enters the playground, the kid should determine the position of which one of the two see-saws he or she wants to inspect and possibly change. Nobody except Eve or Adam will change the positions of the sea-saws during the game.
>
> Afterwards, the kid will be led back to the palace, and I will continue selecting one kid at a time and lead her or him to the playground. Notice that, for example, I may select Eve twice before selecting Adam once. Each kid will visit the playground at most three times.
>
> Before the game starts, I will choose for each kid a color which can be either *green* or *blue* and will tell the chosen color to the kid. I may choose for Adam and Eve the same color or may choose different colors. Eve will not know Adam's color, and Adam will not know Eve's color.

Each kid must choose a color which can again be either green or blue, after visiting the playground at most three times. Each kid must choose a color, regardless of how many times the other kid has visited the playground. A kid may choose a color after visiting the playground less than three times. Once a kid has chosen a color, the kid will not visit the playground after that.

There are two requirements:

1. Adam and Eve must choose the same color, and

2. the color they choose must be one of the colors that I have chosen for them.

Thus, for example, if I choose the color blue for Eve and also blue for Adam then both Adam and Eve must choose blue. Choose wisely!

You will have one chance now to confer with each other and devise a plan. After that, you will be kept in separate rooms in the palace and have no chance at further verbal communication.

You should assume that the positions of the see-saws will both be "left-side-down" to begin with."

The kids came up with a plan using only the see-saws to communicate. Using their plan, they will be able to choose with absolute certainty a color that will satisfy the two requirements. What is the plan?

9.2 APPLICATIONS

Finding a plan for the green-or-blue game amounts to solving a simple version of a classical and important problem for computers, called *agreement* (or *consensus*), using only two shared bits. A bit is a location in memory that at any time can hold one of two values, 0 or 1.

The *agreement problem* is to design an algorithm (i.e., find a strategy) in which all correct processors (or computers) reach a common decision based on their initial opinions. As already explained in Chapters 4 and 5, where processors communicate by sending and receiving messages, the agreement problem is a fundamental coordination problem and is at the core of many algorithms for fault-tolerant distributed applications.

Many applications of an agreement algorithm are discussed in Chapters 4 and 5, and we will not repeat them here. We only mention that one important application is the ability to use an agreement algorithm, on-the-fly, for the election of a coordinator or leader. The leader can initiate some global action, or decide who can use shared resources at any given time.

More important than the algorithms presented in this chapter are the impossibility results discussed in Sections 9.8, 9.9, and 9.10 that identify certain models in which the agreement problem is not solvable.

9.3   TWO OBSERVATIONS

Since Adam and Eve cannot communicate verbally, the only way for them to communicate is by changing the positions of the see-saws. Recall that, at the playground, a kid is allowed to check the position of *only one* see-saw and then may change the position of that see-saw.

First, the kids have observed that it is easy to design a plan for Adam and Eve using *three* see-saws instead of just two. Assume that the initial positions of the three see-saws are "left-side-down." Each kid uses one see-saw to announce her or his initial color (Eve uses the first see-saw and Adam uses the second see-saw), and later each one of them tries to change the position of the third see-saw. The color they both choose is the initial color of the kid that is the first to change the position of the third see-saw.

They have also observed that it is easy to design a plan if the kids were allowed to check the positions of both see-saws and then to change one of them. In such a case, the first kid to enter the playground, say Eve, sees that both see-saws are in their initial positions. She uses one see-saw to announce her initial color and chooses this color (if her initial color is green she changes the position of see-saw #1, otherwise she changes the position of see-saw #2). When Adam later enters the playground, he notices that the one see-saw is not in its initial position, and finds out what is Eve's initial color and chooses this color. In fact, this plan would work for any number of kids, not just two!

9.4   THE KIDS' PLAN

Recall that both see-saws are in the "left-side-down" position to begin with. The kids have devised the following plan to resolve the queen's challenge. Each kid changes the position of the see-saws according to the following strategy.

First visit: The kid checks the position of see-saw #1. If the position is right-side-down, then the kid chooses the blue color and exits the playground. If the position is left-side-down and the kid's initial color is blue, the kid changes the position of see-saw #1 to right-side-down. If the position is left-side-down and the kid's initial color is green, the kid does nothing.

Second visit: The kid checks the position of see-saw #2. If the position is left-side-down, then the kid changes the position of see-saw #2 to right-side-down, chooses her own initial color (i.e., the color chosen for her by the queen), and exits the playground. Otherwise, when the position is right-side-down, the kid does nothing.

Third visit: The kid checks the position of see-saw #1. If the position is left-side-down, then the kid chooses the green color and exits the playground. Otherwise, if the kid's initial color is green, the kid chooses the blue color, and if the kid's initial color is blue, the kid chooses the green color.

This completes the description of the kids' plan.

A SOLUTION FOR THE GREEN-OR-BLUE GAME FOR TWO PLAYERS

Assumptions:

The initial color of the player is $v \in \{green, blue\}$.

Both see-saws are in the "left-side-down" position to begin with

1 **if** *see-saw1 = right-side-down* **then** *choose(blue)*   // `first visit`
      else if $v = blue$ **then** *see-saw1 ← right-side-down*

2 **if** *see-saw2 = left-side-down* **then** {*see-saw2 ← right-side-down;*   // `second visit`
      if $v = blue$ **then** *choose(blue)* **else** *choose(green)*}

3 **if** *see-saw1 = left-side-down* **then** *choose(green)*   // `third visit`
      else if $v = blue$ **then** *choose(green)* **else** *choose(blue)*

Figure 9.1: A plan for a player with initial color $v \in \{green, blue\}$. After choosing a color the player immediately exits the playground.

The code is given in Figure 9.1. This and the other code segments in this chapter can be skipped without loss of continuity.

9.5   FURTHER EXPLANATIONS

We prove below that the kids' plan indeed solves the green-or-blue game. Assume without loss of generality that Eve is the first to enter the playground and to check the position of see-saw #1. There are three possible cases.

Case 1: Eve's initial color is blue.

- Since Eve changes the position of see-saw #1 to right-side-down, during Adam's first visit he finds that the position of see-saw #1 is right-side-down, he chooses blue, exits the playground and never enters it again.

- When Eve finds, during her second visit, that the position of see-saw #2 is left-side-down, she will also choose blue.

Case 2: Eve's initial color is green and Eve changes the position of see-saw #2 to right-side-down first.

- In this case, Eve chooses green.

- Once Adam finds that the position of see-saw #2 is right-side-down, he checks the position of see-saw #1 again.

- We notice that at this point (since Eve did not change the position of see-saw #1) if the position of see-saw #1 is left-side-down then Adam's color is green, and if the position of see-saw #1 is right-side-down then Adam's color is blue.

- If the position of see-saw #1 is left-side-down, then Adam chooses green, agreeing with Eve. If the position of see-saw #1 is right-side-down (which implies that the initial color of Adam is blue), then Adam chooses green, again agreeing with Eve.

Case 3: Eve's initial color is green, and Adam changes the position of see-saw #2 to right-side-down first.

- In this case, Adam chooses his initial color.

- Once Eve finds that the position of see-saw #2 is right-side-down, she checks the position of see-saw #1 again.

- At this point (since Eve did not change the position of see-saw #1) if the position of see-saw #1 is left-side-down then Adam's color is green, and if the position of see-saw #1 is right-side-down then Adam's color is blue.

- If the position of see-saw #1 is left-side-down (which implies that the initial color of Adam is green), then Eve chooses green, agreeing with Adam. If the position of see-saw #1 is right-side-down (which implies that the initial color of Adam is blue), then Eve chooses blue (the color different then her initial color), again agreeing with Adam.

This completes the proof.

9.6   AN ALTERNATIVE PLAN

"I am always surprised," said the queen to the kids after hearing their plan, "that most of the kids that ever solved the green-and-blue game came with the same cumbersome plan as yours. There is a simpler solution in which each kid accesses each one of the two see-saws *at most once*. Try to discover this alternative solution."

Recall that both see-saws are in the "left-side-down" position to begin with. The kids have devised the following alternative plan to resolve the queen's challenge. Each kid changes the position of the see-saws according to the following strategy.

Plan for a kid with initial color green:

- *First visit*: The kid checks the position of see-saw #1. If the position is right-side-down, the kid chooses the green color. If the position is left-side-down, the kid changes the position to right-side-down.

ALTERNATIVE SOLUTION FOR THE GREEN-OR-BLUE GAME FOR TWO PLAYERS

Assumptions:

The initial color of the player is $v \in \{green, blue\}$.

Both see-saws are in the "left-side-down" position to begin with

```
1  if v = green then
2      if see-saw1 = right-side-down then choose(green)                              // first
3          else see-saw1 ← right-side-down
4      if see-saw2 = left-side-down then {see-saw2 ← right-side-down; choose(green)} // second
5          else choose(blue)
6  else                                                                             // v = blue
7      if see-saw2 = left-side-down then {see-saw2 ← right-side-down; choose(blue)}  // first
8          else see-saw2 = right-side-down
9      if see-saw1 = left-side-down then choose(blue)                               // second
10         else choose(green)
```

Figure 9.2: A plan for a player with initial color $v \in \{green, blue\}$. After choosing a color the player immediately exits the playground.

- *Second visit*: The kid checks the position of see-saw #2. If the position is left-side-down, the kid changes the position to right-side-down and chooses green. Otherwise, the kid chooses blue.

Plan for a kid with initial color blue:

- *First visit*: The kid checks the position of see-saw #2. If the position is left-side-down, the kid changes the position to right-side-down and chooses blue.

- *Second visit*: The kid checks the position of see-saw #1. If the position is left-side-down, the kid chooses blue. Otherwise, the kid chooses green.

If the initial color of both players is green then clearly both players would choose green. Similarly, if the initial color of both players is blue then clearly both player would choose blue. If the players do not have the same initial color, the initial color of the player who is the first to change the position of see-saw #2 is chosen. The code of the alternative plan is given in Figure 9.2.

9.7   THE QUEEN'S NEW CHALLENGE

After the kids have solved the queen's challenge, she has presented to them the following new challenge: In the description of the green-or-blue game it is assumed that at the playground the kid was allowed to check the position of one see-saw and then possibly change the position of that see-saw, or leave the see-saw unchanged. In the new challenge the queen has weakened the *communication model* as follows: During each visit to the playground the kid is now allowed to choose *one* of the following three options.

1. As before, check the position of see-saw #1 and then possibly change the position of see-saw #1. The kid may leave see-saw #1 unchanged.

2. Check the position of see-saw #2.
   This option does not allow the kid to change the position of see-saw #2!

3. Change the position of see-saw #2.
   This option does not allow the kid first to check the position of see-saw #2!

Before a kid enters the playground, the kid should select one of the three possible options. The queen has asked the kids to find a plan assuming this new weaker communication model.

Recall that both see-saws are in the "left-side-down" position to begin with. The kids have devised the following plan to resolve the queen's new challenge. Each kid changes the position of the see-saws according to the following strategy.

Plan for a kid with initial color green:

- *First visit*: The kid changes the position of see-saw #1 to right-side-down.

- *Second visit*: The kid checks the position of see-saw #2.
  If the position is left-side-down, the kid chooses green.

- *Third visit*: The kid checks the position of see-saw #1.
  If the position is left-side-down, the kid chooses green. Otherwise, the kid chooses blue.

Plan for a kid with initial color blue:

- *First visit*: The kid changes the position of see-saw #2 to right-side-down.

- *Second visit*: The kid checks the position of see-saw #1. If the position is left-side-down, the kid chooses blue. Otherwise, the kid changes the position to left-side-down, and chooses green.

If both kids have the same color then clearly they will choose that color as either see-saw #1 or see-saw #2 is not updated and is always in the "left-side-down" position. When the kids have different colors, either (1) one kid is faster and chooses a value without noticing that the other kid "is around" and in this case the common chosen value is that of the fast kid, or (2) both kids try to inspect&update see-saw #1, and the common chosen value is the initial color of the *last* (second) kid that tried to inspect&update see-saw#1. The code of the new algorithm is given in Figure 9.3.

Assumptions:
The initial color of the player is $v \in \{green, blue\}$.
Both see-saws are in the "left-side-down" position to begin with

```
1  if v = green then
2      see-saw1 ← right-side-down                              // update without inspect
3      if see-saw2 = left-side-down then choose(green)   // no rival; inspect without update
4      else                                                    // atomic inspect&update step
5          if see-saw1 = left-side-down           // lines 5-7 are executed as one atomic step
6          then choose(green)                          // the "blue kid" changed it back first
7          else {see-saw1 ← left-side-down; choose(blue)}        // I changed it back first
8  else                                                                    // v = blue
9      see-saw2 ← right-side-down                              // update without inspect
10     if see-saw1 = left-side-down         // inspect&update: lines 10-12 are an atomic step
11     then choose(blue)                    // no rival or the "green kid" changed it back first
12     else {see-saw1 ← left-side-down; choose(green)}           // I changed it back first
```

Figure 9.3: A plan for a player with initial color $v \in \{green, blue\}$. After choosing a color the player immediately exits the playground.

9.8   A SURPRISING IMPOSSIBILITY RESULT

The next question that comes to mind after solving the queen's new challenge is whether it is possible to weaken the communication model further and still solve the green-or-blue game.

Assume the communication model is weakened as follows. During each visit to the playground the kid is now allowed to choose *one* of the following *four* options:

1. Check the position of see-saw #1.
   This option does not allow the kid to change the position of see-saw #1!

2. Change the position of see-saw #1.
   This option does not allow the kid first to check the position of see-saw #1!

3. Check the position of see-saw #2.
   This option does not allow the kid to change the position of see-saw #2!

4. Change the position of see-saw #2.
   This option does not allow the kid first to check the position of see-saw #2!

Before a kid enters the playground, the kid should select one of the four possible options. It is surprising and very interesting to find out that, under the new assumption, it is not possible to devise a winning strategy (i.e., a plan) for the game! In fact, it is possible to prove the following stronger result.

> There is no winning strategy for the green-or-blue game when it is played with two players, even if instead of two see-saws there are as many see-saws as the players may like in the playground, and instead of allowing each player to enter the playground at most three times, each player may enter the playground at most k times where k is a natural number that can be as big as the players like. However, the value for k should be decided upon before the game starts.

The assumption that the value of k—the number of times each player may enter the playground—should be decided upon before the game starts is essential for proving the impossibility result. If we allow each player to access the playground unlimited number of times, then it is easy to devise a simple plan for any number of players using two see-saws only. Such a plan is described below.

The kids elect one of them as the leader, say Eve. In her first visit, Eve uses see-saw #1 to announce her initial color (if her initial color is green she leaves see-saw #1 in the left-side-down position, otherwise she changes its position to right-side-down). Then, in her second visit, she changes the position of see-saw #2 letting everybody know that a decision has been made, and chooses her initial color. Every other kid waits until the position of see-saw #2 changes from its initial (known) position and then, after examining the position of see-saw #1, finds out what is Eve's initial color and also chooses this color. The above impossibility result is a special case of a general result discussed in Section 9.10.

9.9   THE QUEEN'S FINAL CHALLENGE

Before the kids left, the queen has asked them a challenging question that they can try to solve back home. The queen has described her challenge as follows.

> "So far, you have had to devise a plan—a winning strategy—in order to solve my questions. This time I am going to ask you to prove that there is no winning strategy for solving the following question. Consider the original version of the green-or-blue game from Section 9.1 (page 73) where, at every visit, a kid is allowed to check the position of one see-saw and then may change the position of that see-saw. We have played this game with only two players. Prove that it is not possible to devise a winning strategy for this game when it is played with three players instead of just two.
>
> In fact, try to prove the following stronger result. There is no winning strategy for the green-or-blue game when it is played with three players, even if instead of two see-saws there are as many see-saws as you may like in the playground, and instead of allowing each

player to enter the playground at most three times, each player may enter the playground at most k times where k is a natural number that can be as big as you like. However, the value for k should be decided upon before the game starts.

It is assumed that the positions of the see-saws are all "left-side-down" to begin with. I emphasize again, that at the playground a kid is allowed to check the position of one see-saw only and then may change the position of that see-saw.

This is my final challenge to you, and it is a very difficult one."

We point out that the assumption in the queen's challenge that the value of k—the number of times each player may enter the playground—should be decided upon before the game starts, is essential for proving the impossibility result. If we allow each player to access the playground unlimited number of times, then the plan mentioned in the last paragraph of Section 9.8 solves the problem for any number of players using two see-saws only.

The impossibility results of Section 9.8 and Section 9.9 would still hold when the requirement that each player may enter the playground at most k times where k is a natural number that should be decided upon before the game starts, is replaced with the following weaker requirement: Each kid has to eventually decide after entering the playground a finite number of times, even if any number of the other kids, from some point on never get a chance to enter the playground.[1]

9.10   GENERAL IMPOSSIBILITY RESULTS

The impossibility results mentioned in Sections 9.8 and 9.9 are special cases of more general impossibility results, which imply that a group of processors (or computers) cannot reach agreement on one of two values, in the presence of process failures, when the communication medium is too restricted. These general results are stated below using some basic computer science terminology. In all the results below, we assume a distributed *asynchronous* system—a system where no assumption is made about the (relative) "speed" of the processors.

READ/WRITE REGISTERS

An *atomic read/write register* (atomic register for short) is a shared memory location that can hold a value, where a processor can atomically either read the value of the shared register or update the value of the shared register. Between the time a processor finishes reading and starts writing, some other processor may access the register, and possibly change its value. An atomic *bit* is an atomic register which can hold only the values 0 and 1.

An atomic bit corresponds to a single see-saw that can be in one of two positions, where the position of the see-saw can either be inspected (i.e., read) in one atomic step or modified (i.e., written) in one atomic step. However, it cannot be inspected and modified in a single atomic step.

---

[1]A kid that from some point on never gets a chance to enter the playground corresponds to a processor that *fails by crashing*, that is, a processor that stops its execution.

Thus, the following impossibility result, which was already mentioned in Section 4.4 (page 26) implies the impossibility result mentioned in Section 9.8 (page 80).

> There is no agreement algorithm for two or more processors (or computers) that can tolerate even a single process crash failure (in an asynchronous system) where communication is done by reading and writing atomic registers.

Let us explain all the notions that are mentioned in the above statement. As already explained, an *agreement* algorithm (also called consensus algorithm) is a plan (a strategy) for processors to reach a common decision based on their initial opinions. The decision value must be the initial opinion of some processor; thus, when all processors are unanimous in their initial opinions, the decision value must be the common opinion. All the impossibility results in this chapter also hold for *binary* agreement where there are only two possible decision values. A processor that *fails by crashing* is a processor that stops its execution. A crashed processor corresponds to a kid that from some point on never gets a chance to enter the playground.

The above result is one of the most known impossibility result in distributed computing and it implies a similar result for asynchronous message passing systems. This follows from the simple observation that a shared memory system which supports atomic read/write registers can simulate a message passing system which supports send and receive operations. The simulation is as follows. With each process p we associate an unbounded array of shared registers which all processes can read from but only p can write into. To simulate the sending of a message, p writes to the next unused register in its associated array. When p has to receive a message, it reads from each process all the new messages.

READ-MODIFY-WRITE BITS

An atomic *read-modify-write bit* is a shared object which all the processors may access, that can hold the values 0 or 1. A processor can atomically read the value of the shared bit and then based on the value read, compute some new value (i.e., 0 or 1) and assign it back to the bit. By *atomic* we mean that while a processor is accessing the bit, no other processor can also access it. *A read-modify-write bit corresponds to a single see-saw* that can be in one of two positions, where the position of the see-saw can be inspected and modified in one atomic step! Thus, the following impossibility result implies the impossibility result mentioned in Section 9.9.

> There is no agreement algorithm for three or more processors (or computers) using any number of atomic read-modify-write bits and using any number of atomic read/write registers, if two or more processors can fail by crashing.

As the queen has already pointed out, proving such a result is rather difficult.

QUEUES AND STACKS

A shared queue is a data structure that supports *enqueue* and *dequeue* operations, by several processes. The enqueue operation inserts a value into the queue and the dequeue operation returns and removes the oldest value in the queue. If the queue is empty, the dequeue operation returns a special symbol. A shared stack is a data structure that supports *push* and *pop* operations, by several processes. The push operation inserts a value into the stack and the pop operation returns and removes the newest value in the stack. If the stack is empty, the push operation returns a special symbol.

> *There is no agreement algorithm for three or more processors using any number of shared queues (resp. stacks) and using any number of atomic read/write registers, if two or more processors can fail by crashing.*

In the kids' plan presented in Section 9.7, it is possible to replace see-saw #1 with either a queue, a stack or a read-modify-write bit, and it is possible to replace see-saw #2 with an atomic read/write bit. This means that it is possible to solve agreement for two processes in the presence of a single crash failure using a queue, a stack or an atomic read-modify-write bit, together with an atomic read/write bit.

IMPLICATIONS

The *consensus number* of a shared object (like a read-modify-write bit) is the largest n for which, in an asynchronous system, it is possible to solve consensus (i.e., agreement) for n processors using any number of objects of that type and any number of atomic registers. It is required that in the solution one processor is not able to prevent another processor from reaching a decision, and thus the solution should be able to tolerate an arbitrary number of processor (crash) failures.

Since, in an asynchronous system, it is not possible to solve agreement for three processors in the presence of two crash failures using a queue, a stack or an atomic read-modify-write bit, together with an atomic read/write bit, but it is possible to do so for two processors, it follows that the consensus number of a read-modify-write bit, a queue and a stack is exactly 2.

At the beginning of the section (and also in Section 4.4) we have mentioned that there is no agreement algorithm for two or more processors using any number of atomic read/write registers, if one or more processors can fail by crashing. Thus, the consensus number of a read/write register is 1. Since the consensus number of a read-modify-write bit, a queue and a stack is 2, the following is true.

> *For two (or more) processors, it is not possible to implement a single read-modify-write bit, a single queue, or a single stack using any number of atomic read/write registers assuming a single processor may fail!*

Classifying objects by their consensus numbers is a powerful technique for understanding the relative power of shared objects. Modern multi-processor (and also uni-processor) architectures support powerful shared objects. Observations made about the consensus numbers of various shared objects help in deciding whether these objects are sufficient for implementing important algorithms and data structures.

9.11   CHAPTER NOTES

The agreement problem was formally defined by Marshall Pease, Robert Shostak, and Leslie Lamport in [38]. The plan presented in Section 9.4 (page 75) is based on an algorithm by Michael C. Loui and H. Abu-Amara presented in [35]. The plan presented in Section 9.6 (page 77) is based on an algorithm suggested by Amir Taubenfeld.

On page 84, it is written that "In the kids' plan presented in Section 9.7, it is possible to replace see-saw #1 with either a queue, a stack or a read-modify-write bit, and it is possible to replace see-saw #2 with an atomic read/write bit." Such an algorithm that uses a single queue and an atomic bit, due to Roy Ramon (2005), can be found on page 317 of [48].

The two impossibility results (1) for atomic registers, and (2) for read-modify-write bits presented in Section 9.10 are from [35]. A version of the proof of the impossibility result for atomic registers from [35] can be found on page 318 of [48]. The impossibility result for queues and stacks presented in Section 9.10 is from [27]. The notion of a consensus number was introduced by Maurice P. Herlihy as a measure for the computational power of shared objects [27].

The power of various shared objects has been studied extensively in shared memory environments where processes may fail benignly, and where every operation is wait-free. Objects that can be used, together with atomic registers, to build wait-free implementations of any other object are called *universal objects* [27, 40]. Consensus objects are known to be universal [27].

9.12   SELF REVIEW

Questions:

1. Is it important that in all the plans presented in this chapter, the initial position of both see-saw #1 and see-saw #2 are *a priori* known?

2. Show that the green-or-blue game can be solved for any (*a priori* known) number of players using three see-saws, assuming that: (1) at the playground a player is allowed to check the position of all the three see-saws and then change any number of them; (2) each player can access the playground an unlimited number of times; (3) the players do not know which position the three see-saws are in to begin with; and (4) all players must follow exactly the same rules, in particular, it is not allowed to designate one player as a leader who will behave differently than others. (This is a difficult question.)

3. Consider the original version of the green-or-blue game from Section 9.1 (page 73), where a kid is allowed to check the position of a see-saw and then may change the position of that see-saw. Is it possible to solve the green-or-blue game for two players using only a *single* see-saw (instead of two see-saws) assuming that there is no limit on how many times a player may enter the playground?

Answers:

1. Yes.

2. Hint: use the solution for the see-saw puzzle from Chapter 8.

3. No.

CHAPTER 10

Getting the Service You Deserve

We look at the problem of guaranteeing that up to ℓ customers and no more may simultaneously access identical copies of the same type of a resource when there are more than ℓ competing customers. A solution is required to withstand the possible *failure by crashing* (i.e., death) of up to $\ell-1$ customers. By a failure of a customer, we simply mean that the customer stops participating in the algorithm, without notifying anybody. The problem of efficiently utilizing the resources by giving the customers the best service possible under the given limitations is expressed abstractly as the *two tellers problem*.[1]

10.1 THE TWO TELLERS PROBLEM

To illustrate the problem, consider a bank where customers are waiting for tellers. Here the resources are the tellers, and the parameter ℓ is the number of tellers. We notice that the usual bank solution, where customers line up in a single queue, and the customer at the head of the queue goes to any free teller, is problematic for several reasons. If $\ell \geq 2$ tellers are free, a proper solution should enable the first ℓ customers in line to move simultaneously to a teller. However, the bank solution, requires them to move past the head of the queue one at a time. Moreover, if the customer at the front of the line "fails," then the customers behind this customer wait forever.

Thus, a better solution is required which will not allow a single failure to tie up all the resources. Below we present such a better solution, but first we need to accurately define the two tellers problem.

It is assumed that there are exactly *two* tellers and exactly *three* customers. The customers are named Alice, Bob, and Carol, and they can come to the bank in order to get service from tellers as often as they like. Inside the bank there is a board on top of which they can leave notes and remove them later. Alice, Bob, and Carol cannot see each other and they communicate with each other only by writing and reading of notes. In particular, Alice cannot see that Bob, and Carol are reading a note that she has written earlier. So, Alice, Bob, and Carol are looking for a solution to ensure the following.

[1]It is recommended to read Chapter 2 before reading Chapter 10.

1. *Each one of the two tellers serves at most one customer at any given time.*

2. *If at most one customer may fail[2] while waiting to be served or while being served by a teller, and some other customer wants to be served, then eventually some other customer will be served by a teller.*

The first requirement ensures that at most one customer will go to a free teller to get service at any given time. The second requirement ensures that a single failure will not tie up all the resources.

Notice that we do not require that when some customer, say Alice, wants to be served and she never fails then eventually she will be served. We only require that if Alice wants to be served then eventually somebody will be served. Furthermore, a proper solution should ensure that, if someone wants to be served, then someone will be served even if only one customer shows up.

10.2   APPLICATIONS

To see the corresponding synchronization problem for computers, replace the two *tellers* with two *printers* (i.e., the two resources), and let Alice, Bob, and Carol be the names of three computers that are trying to avoid using the same printer at the same time. More generally, we are trying to implement a concurrent queue data structure which, unlike in a conventional queue, ensures that a failure of an element in the queue will not block other elements.

The two tellers problem is a special case of the ℓ-*exclusion* problem, which is to find an algorithm which guarantees that up to ℓ computers (or processors) and no more may simultaneously access identical copies of the same non-sharable resource when there are several competing computers. A solution is required to withstand the slow-down or even the crash (fail by stopping) of up to $\ell-1$ computers.

Finally, the customers who communicate only by writing and reading of notes correspond to computers (or processors) which communicate either by writing and reading shared memory registers or by sending and receiving messages.

10.3   FIRST ATTEMPT: A SOLUTION WHICH CANNOT TOLERATE A SINGLE FAULT

For this solution, three labeled notes are used. Alice uses a note labeled A, Bob uses a note labeled B, and Carol uses a note labeled C.

Alice: When Alice enters the bank:

1. She leaves a note labeled A on the board.

---

[2]That is, stop participating without notifying anybody (die).

2. Then, if she finds that there is a note labeled B, she checks the board over and over again waiting for Bob to remove his note. Once Alice finds that there is a note labeled B, she continues to the next step below.

3. She checks if there is a note labeled C, and if she finds that there is a note labeled C, she checks the board over and over again waiting also for Carol to remove her note. Once Alice finds that there is no note labeled C, she continues to the next step below.

4. She goes to a free teller.[3] After she gets the service she needs, she removes note A.

Bob: When Bob enters the bank:

1. He leaves a note labeled B on the board.

2. Then, if he finds that there is a note labeled A, he does the following:

   (*a*) removes note B;

   (*b*) checks the board over and over again until there is no note labeled A; and

   (*c*) goes back to step 1 above and starts all over again.

   Otherwise (if Bob finds that there is no note labeled A, in which case there must be a note labeled B), he continues to the next step below.

3. He checks if there is a note labeled C. If he finds that there is a note labeled C, he checks the board over and over again waiting for Carol to remove her note. Once Bob finds that there is no note labeled C, he continues to the next step below.

4. He goes to a free teller. After he gets the service he needs, he removes note B.

Carol: When Carol enters the bank:

1. She leaves a note labeled C on the board.

2. Then, if she finds that there is either a note labeled A or a note labeled B, she does the following:

   (*a*) removes note C;

   (*b*) checks the board over and over again until there is no note labeled A;

   (*c*) checks the board over and over again until there is no note labeled B; and

   (*d*) goes back to step 1 above and starts all over again.

---

[3]The details of of how does Alice know which teller is free are irrelevant.

PROGRAM FOR ALICE:	PROGRAM FOR BOB:	PROGRAM FOR CAROL:
1 leave A	1 **repeat**	1 **repeat**
2 **wait** (no B)	2 leave B	2 leave C
3 **wait** (no C)	3 **if** A {	3 **if** (A or B) {
4 go to a free teller	4 remove B	4 remove C
5 remove A	5 **wait** (no A)}	5 **wait** (no A)
	6 **until** B	6 **wait** (no B)}
	7 **wait** (no C)	7 **until** C
	8 go to a free teller	8 go to a free teller
	9 remove B	9 remove C

Figure 10.1: The code for the first attempt. The algorithm cannot tolerate even a single fault. The statement "wait (no A)" means *wait until* there is no note labeled A posted on the shared board.

Otherwise (if Carol finds that there is no note labeled A and no note labeled B, in which case there must be a note labeled C), she continues to the next step below.

3. She goes to a free teller. After she gets the service she needs, she removes note C.

The code is given in Figure 10.1. This and the other code segment in this chapter can be skipped without loss of continuity. "if A" means if there is a note labeled A, "wait (no A)" means *wait until* there is no note labeled A,[4] "until B" means, continue with the following statement only if Bob's note is currently posted, otherwise go back to the repeat statement and start again.

The above solution does *not* satisfy the second requirement. Assume that Alice arrives at the bank first, leaves a note labeled *A*, and (unfortunately) fails. Once Bob and Carol arrive they will forever wait for Alice to remove her note.

However, the above solution does guarantee that: (1) at any point in time only one customer can get service from each one of the two tellers; and (2) if some customer wants to be served, then eventually some customer will be served by a teller, provided that nobody fail. Thus, interestingly, this solution is a correct solution to the "too much bread" problem from Chapter 2, for *three* participants! Simply replace the statement "go to a free teller" with "if there is no bread, buy bread." Unlike the correct solution for two participants in Section 10.2, this solution is *not* symmetric: Alice has a better chance than Bob to go and buy bread, and Bob has a better chance than Carol to go and buy bread.

---

[4]"wait (no A)" is equivalent to the statement "while A {skip}." It is implemented by repeatedly testing whether note A is posted, a method which is called *busy waiting*.

10.4   SECOND ATTEMPT: A CORRECT SOLUTION

For this solution, four labeled notes are used. Alice uses a note labeled *A*, Bob uses two notes labeled *B1* and *B2*, and Carol uses a note labeled *C*.

Alice: When Alice enters the bank:

1. She leaves a note labeled A on the board.

2. Next, she checks the board over and over again until either there is no note labeled B1 or there is no note labeled C.

3. Then, if she finds that there is both a note labeled B2 and a note labeled C, she goes back to step 2 above and starts all over again. Otherwise (if Alice finds that there is either no note labeled B2 or no note labeled C), she continues to the next step below.

4. She goes to a free teller. After she gets the service she needs, she removes note A.

Bob: When Bob enters the bank:

1. He leaves a note labeled B1 on the board.

2. Then, he checks the board over and over again until either there is no note labeled A or there is no note labeled C.

3. Next, he leaves a note labeled B2 on the board.

4. Then, if he finds that there is both a note labeled A and a note labeled C, he does the following:

    (*a*) removes note B2; and

    (*b*) goes back to step 2 above and starts all over again.

    Otherwise (if Bob finds that there is either no note labeled A or no note labeled C, in which case there must be a note labeled B2), he continues to the next step below.

5. He goes to a free teller. After he gets the service he needs, he first removes note B2, and only then he removes note B1.

Carol: When Carol enters the bank:

1. She checks the board over and over again until there is either no note labeled A or no note labeled B1.

2. Next, she leaves a note labeled C on the board.

PROGRAM FOR ALICE:

```
1 leave A
2 repeat
3     wait ((no B1) or (no C))
4 until ((no B2) or (no C))
5 go to a free teller
6 remove A
```

PROGRAM FOR BOB:

```
1   leave B1
2   repeat
3       wait ((no A) or (no C))
4       leave B2
5       if (A and C) {
6           remove B2}
7   until B2
8   go to a free teller
9   remove B2
10 remove B1
```

PROGRAM FOR CAROL:

```
1 repeat
2     wait ((no A) or (no B1))
3     leave C
4     if (A and B2) {
5         remove C}
6 until C
7 go to a free teller
8 remove C
```

Figure 10.2: The code for the second attempt. A correct algorithm.

3. Then, if she finds that there is both a note labeled A and a note labeled B2, she does the following:

   (*a*) removes note C; and

   (*b*) goes back to step 1 above and starts all over again.

   Otherwise (if Carol finds that there is either no note labeled A or no note labeled B2, in which case there must be a note labeled C), she continues to the next step below.

4. She goes to a free teller. After she gets the service she needs, she removes note C.

The code is given in Figure 10.2.

The above solution does satisfies the two requirements: (1) each one of the two tellers serves at most one customer at any give time; and (2) as long as at most one customer fails, and some other customer wants to be served, then eventually some other customer will be served by a teller. We notice that this solution is *not* symmetric: Alice has a better chance of being served than Bob, and Bob has a better chance of being served than Carol.

10.5   HOW MANY NOTES ARE NEEDED?

The number of notes used in the correct two tellers algorithm is four (i.e., A, B1, B2, C) for three customers and two tellers. What is the minimal number of notes necessary? It has been shown that the problem *cannot* be solved using only one note, labeled with the customer name, per customer. That is four notes are necessary and sufficient in this case. In fact, the following much stronger result, which for any ℓ and n, provides a tight space bound on the number of labeled notes (bits) required to solve the generalization of the two tellers problem for n customers and ℓ tellers, is known.

- *A lower bound.* For any $\ell \geq 2$ and $n > \ell$, every algorithm which solves the generalization of the two tellers problem for n customers (processors) and ℓ tellers (resources) must use at least $2n - 2$ labeled notes (bits): at least two notes per customers for $n - 2$ of the customers and at least one note per customer for the remaining two customers.

- *A matching upper bound.* For $\ell \geq 2$ and $n > \ell$, there is an algorithm which solves the generalization of the two tellers problem for n customers (processors)) and ℓ tellers (resources) that uses $2n - 2$ labeled notes (bits): two notes per customer for $n - 2$ of the customers and one bit per customer for the remaining two customers.

It follows from the above results that it is not possible to solve the problem for n customers and ℓ tellers with one labeled note per customer, for any $n > \ell \geq 2$.

10.6   CHAPTER NOTES

As already mentioned, the two tellers problem is a special case of a problem called the ℓ-*exclusion* problem, which is to find an algorithm which guarantees that up to ℓ computing devices and no more may simultaneously access identical copies of the same resource when there are n competing devices, for any $\ell \geq 1$ and $n \geq 1$. The ℓ-exclusion problem is a generalization of the mutual exclusion problem (mentioned on page 17). Mutual exclusion is the same as 1-exclusion. The ℓ-exclusion problem was first defined and solved by Michael J. Fischer, Nancy A. Lynch, James E. Burns, and Allan Borodin in [19].

The correct algorithm presented on page 91 is derived from an algorithm that works for any number of customers and tellers, which appeared in a paper by Gadi Taubenfeld [49]. The number of notes used in this algorithm—four notes for three customers and two tellers—is the minimal number of notes necessary. The problem *cannot* be solved using only one note per customer. In fact, it is proven in [49] that for $n \geq 2$ customers (processors) and $\ell \geq 2$ tellers (resources) , $2n - 2$ labeled notes (bits) are necessary and sufficient.

The first algorithm presented on page 88 (which cannot tolerate a single fault) is derived from an algorithm that solves the mutual exclusion problem (and the too much bread problem from Chapter 2) for any number of participants, which was first published in a paper by James E. Burns [8].

10.7 SELF REVIEW

Questions:

1. The question refers to the first attempt solution. Assume that nobody fails.

    (a) Does the solution guarantee that if Alice wants to be served then eventually she will be served?

    (b) Does the solution guarantee that if Bob wants to be served then eventually he will be served?

    (c) Does the solution guarantee that if Carol wants to be served then eventually she will be served?

2. The question refers to the second attempt solution. Assume that nobody fails.

    (a) Does the solution guarantee that if Alice wants to be served then eventually she will be served?

    (b) Does the solution guarantee that if Bob wants to be served then eventually he will be served?

    (c) Does the solution guarantee that if Carol wants to be served then eventually she will be served?

Answers:

1(a) & 2(a) Yes. If Alice wants to be served then eventually she will be served.

1(b) & 2(b) No. Alice can bypass Bob infinitely often, preventing Bob from ever being served.

1(c) & 2(c) No. Alice and Bob can bypass Carol infinitely often, preventing Carol from ever being served.

Bibliography

[1] M. K. Aguilera and S. Toueg. A simple bivalency proof that t-resilient consensus requires $t + 1$ rounds. *Information Processing Letters*, 71(3):155–158, 1999. DOI: 10.1016/s0020-0190(99)00100-3.

The authors use a simple bivalency argument to show that in a synchronous system with up to t crash failures solving consensus requires at least $t + 1$ rounds. 29, 38, 97

[2] E. A. Akkoyunlu, K. Ekanadham, and R. V. Huber. Some constraints and tradeoffs in the design of network communications. *SIGOPS Operating Systems Review*, 9(5):67–74, November 1975. Also in *Proc. of the 5th ACM Symposium on Operating Systems Principles*, 1975. DOI: 10.1145/1067629.806523.

A problem is introduced, which is similar to the two lovers problem from Chapter 3, and the coordinated attack problem from [22]. The problem is described on page 21. 21, 98, 99

[3] K. R. Apt. Edsger Wybe Dijkstra (1930–2002): A portrait of a genius. *Formal Aspects of Computing*, 14:92–98, 2002. DOI: 10.1007/s001650200029.

Sections included: Scientific Career, Scientific Contributions, Working Style, His Opinions, Life in Austin, Lifestyle, Legacy. 17

[4] J. Bar-Ilan and D. Peleg. Distributed resource allocation algorithms. In *International Workshop on Distributed Algorithms*, LNCS, Springer Verlag, 1992. DOI: 10.1007/3-540-56188-9_19.

A few algorithms for the dining/drinking philosophers problem are presented in different models of computation and communication in a distributed system. 59

[5] P. Berman and J. A. Garay. Asymptotically optimal distributed consensus (extended abstract). In *Proc. of the 16th International Colloquium on Automata, Languages and Programming (ICALP)*, pages 80–94, 1989. DOI: 10.1007/bfb0035753.

The Byzantine agreement algorithm which appears in Section 5.4 (page 35) is presented. The algorithm achieves agreement with $n > 4t$ processors using $2t + 2$ rounds of communication and messages of constant size. 38

[6] P. A. Bernstein and N. Goodman. Timestamp-based algorithms for concurrency control in distributed database systems. In *Proc. of the International Conference on Very Large*

Databases, pages 285–300, 1980.

Several timestamp-based concurrency-control algorithms are discussed. 59

[7] E. Borowsky and E. Gafni. Generalized FLP impossibility result for *t*-resilient asynchronous computations. In *Proc. of the 25th ACM Symposium on Theory of Computing*, pages 91–100, 1993. DOI: 10.1145/167088.167119.

Among other results, the authors prove the impossibility result for set-consensus as stated on page 29. See also [28, 45]. 29, 99, 101

[8] J. E. Burns. Mutual exclusion with linear waiting using binary shared variables. *SIGACT News*, 10(2):42–47, 1978. DOI: 10.1145/990524.990527.

Upper and lower bounds are proved for solving the mutual exclusion with shared bits and test-and-set bits. 93

[9] J. E. Burns. Complexity of communication among asynchronous parallel processes. *Technical Report GIT-ICS-81/01*, Georgia Institute of Technology, 1981.

The Ph.D. dissertation of Jim Burns. Among many other results, Burns had also presented the LR algorithm for the dining philosophers problem (see page 54). 59

[10] T. A. Cargill. A robust distributed solution to the dining philosophers problem. *Software— Practice and Experience*, 12:965–969, 1982. DOI: 10.1002/spe.4380121009.

The LR algorithm (page 54), which seems to be folklore, is studied. The author observes that it is possible to get into a situation in which only a *quarter* of the philosophers will be able to eat simultaneously when all of them are hungry. 59

[11] K. M. Chandy and J. Misra. The drinking philosophers problem. *ACM Transactions on Programming Languages and Systems*, 6:632–646, 1984. DOI: 10.1145/1780.1804.

The paper extends the dining philosophers problem to an arbitrary graph network, in which a philosopher needs to acquire the resources on some non-empty subset of its incident edges in order to eat; this subset of resources may change over time. 59

[12] S. Chaudhuri. More choices allow more faults: Set consensus problems in totally asynchronous systems. *Information and Computation*, 105(1):132–158, 1993. DOI: 10.1006/inco.1993.1043.

The author has defined the k-set consensus problem (also called k-set agreement). She has shown that the problem has a simple $(k-1)$-resilient algorithm in an asynchronous system, and conjectured that there is no k-resilient algorithm for this problem. 29

[13] E. W. Dijkstra. Solution of a problem in concurrent programming control. *Communications of the ACM*, 8(9):569, 1965. DOI: 10.1145/357980.357989.

A classical paper in which the mutual exclusion problem was first stated. The paper presents the **first** solution to the mutual exclusion problem for *n* processes. It is deadlock-free, but is not starvation-free. 17

[14] E. W. Dijkstra. Co-operating sequential processes. In F. Genuys, Ed., *Programming Languages*, pages 43–112. Academic Press, New York, 1968. Reprinted from *Technical Report EWD-123*, Technological University, Eindhoven, the Netherlands, 1965.

A classical paper by Dijkstra which also discuss Dekker's algorithm—the **first** solution to the mutual exclusion problem for two processes using atomic registers. Also introduces the important notion of a *semaphore*. 6, 59

[15] E. W. Dijkstra. Hierarchical ordering of sequential processes. *Acta Informatica*, 1:115–138, 1971. Also in *Operating Systems Techniques*, C. A. R. Hoare and R. H. Perrott, Eds. Academic Press, 1972. DOI: 10.1007/bf00289519.

Various principles of synchronizing sequential processes are discussed, including: the mutual exclusion problem, semaphores, and the dining philosophers problem. 59

[16] A. Dumas. *The Three Musketeers*. T. Nelson and Sons Limited, 602 pages, 1878.

The 19th-century classic by the French author Alexandre Dumas. 71

[17] K. P. Eswaran, J. N. Gary, A. Lorie, and I. L. Traiger. The notion of consistency and predicate locks in database systems. *Communications of the ACM*, 19(11):624–633, 1976. DOI: 10.1145/360363.360369.

Introduces the two-phase locking algorithm. 59

[18] M. J. Fischer and N. A. Lynch. A lower bound for the time to assure interactive consistency. *Information Processing Letters*, 14(4):183–186, 1982. DOI: 10.1016/0020-0190(82)90033-3.

Prove that in a synchronous system with up to *t* Byzantine failures solving consensus requires at least $t + 1$ rounds. This result follows immediately from the much stronger result for crash failures discussed in Section 4.7 (page 28) [1]. 38

[19] M. J. Fischer, N. A. Lynch, J. E. Burns, and A. Borodin. Resource allocation with immunity to limited process failure. In *Proc. 20th IEEE Symposium on Foundations of Computer Science*, pages 234–254, October 1979. DOI: 10.1109/sfcs.1979.37.

The paper where the ℓ-exclusion problem was first defined and solved. 93

[20] M. J. Fischer, N. A. Lynch, and M. S. Paterson. Impossibility of distributed consensus with one faulty process. *Journal of the ACM*, 32(2):374–382, 1985. DOI: 10.1145/3149.214121.

It is proved that there is no consensus algorithm that can tolerate even a single crash failure in an asynchronous message-passing system. This is one of the most interesting results in the area of distributed computing. See also [35]. 29, 100, 101

[21] M. J. Fischer, S. Moran, S. Rudich, and G. Taubenfeld. The wakeup problem. *SIAM Journal on Computing*, 25(6):1332–1357, 1996. DOI: 10.1137/s0097539793254959.

A new problem called the wakeup problem is presented. Solutions to the problem are presented which can be used to solve consensus, leader-election, and other related problems. It includes the see-saw algorithm presented on page 68. 71

[22] J. Gray. Notes on data base operating systems. *Operating Systems, an Advanced Course*, Lecture Notes in Computer Science, 60:393–481, 1978. Also appeared as *IBM Research Report RJ2188*. DOI: 10.1007/3-540-08755-9_9.

Among other issues, the coordinated attack problem is introduced, which is similar to the two lovers problem from Chapter 3, and the problem from [2]. The problem is described on page 22. 21, 22, 95, 99

[23] D. S. Greenberg, G. Taubenfeld, and Da-Wei Wang. Choice coordination with multiple alternatives (preliminary version). In *Proc. of the 6th International Workshop on Distributed Algorithms*, 1992. *LNCS 647*, pages 54–68, Springer Verlag 1992. DOI: 10.1007/3-540-56188-9_4.

The authors characterize when the choice coordination problem with k alternatives can be solved deterministically, prove upper and lower space bounds for deterministic solutions, and provide a randomized algorithm which is significantly better than the deterministic lower bound. 47, 49

[24] R. Guerraoui. Indulgent algorithms. In *Proc. 19th ACM Symposium on Principles of Distributed Computing*, pages 289–298, 2000.

An indulgent algorithm never violates its safety property, and eventually satisfies its liveness property when the synchrony assumptions it relies on are satisfied. Various results regarding algorithms that are indulgent towards their failure detector are presented. See also [25, 47]. 30, 98, 101

[25] R. Guerraoui and M. Raynal. The information structure of indulgent consensus. *IEEE Transactions on Computers*, 53(4):453–466, 2004. DOI: 10.1109/tc.2004.1268403.

The authors present a simple and generic indulgent consensus algorithm, and study the inherent complexity of indulgent consensus. See also [24, 47]. 30, 98, 101

[26] J. Y. Halpern and Y. Moses. Knowledge and common knowledge in a distributed environment. *Journal of the ACM*, 37(3):549–587, 1990. DOI: 10.1145/79147.79161.

A general framework for formalizing and reasoning about knowledge in distributed systems is presented. Includes an impossibility proof for the coordinated attack problem [2, 22]. For example, the two lovers problem from Section 3 (page 19). 21

[27] M. P. Herlihy. Wait-free synchronization. *ACM Transactions on Programming Languages and Systems*, 13(1):124–149, January 1991. DOI: 10.1145/114005.102808.

A hierarchy of objects such that no object at one level has a wait-free implementation in terms of objects at lower levels is introduced, and the universality of consensus is proved. 85

[28] M. P. Herlihy and N. Shavit. The topological structure of asynchronous computability. *Journal of the ACM*, 46(6):858–923, July 1999. DOI: 10.1145/331524.331529.

Among other results, the authors prove the impossibility result for set-consensus as stated on page 29. See also [7, 45]. 29, 96, 101

[29] H. Jordan. A special purpose architecture for finite element analysis. In *Proc. of the International Conference on Parallel Processing*, pages 263–266, 1978.

Considers barrier synchronization in parallel algorithms. 71

[30] J. L. W. Kessels. Arbitration without common modifiable variables. *Acta Informatica*, 17(2):135–141, June 1982. DOI: 10.1007/bf00288966.

A two-process mutual exclusion algorithm, based on Peterson's algorithm [39], is presented which uses single-writer atomic registers. The algorithm is generalized for any arbitrary number of competitors by applying the binary solution in a binary arbitration tree. 17

[31] J. F. Kurose and K. W. Ross. *Computer Networking: A Top-Down Approach*, 7th ed., Pearson, 2016, 864 pages.

There is an emphasis on application-layer paradigms (the top layer), encouraging understanding and experience with protocols and networking concepts, before working down the Internet protocol stack to the lower layers. 6

[32] L. Lamport. The part-time parliament. *ACM Transactions on Computer Systems*, 16(2):133–169, May 1998. DOI: 10.1145/279227.279229.

The Paxos algorithm is presented. At the heart of the algorithm is a three-phase consensus protocol. The paper won an ACM SIGOPS Hall of Fame Award in 2012. 30

[33] L. Lamport, R. Shostak, and M. Pease. The Byzantine generals problem. *ACM Transactions on Programming Languages and Systems*, 4(3):382–401, July 1982. DOI: 10.1145/357172.357176.

Introduced and solved the Byzantine Generals problem defined in Section 5.1 (page 33). The results are related to those from [38] where the agreement problem was first defined. 38, 100

[34] D. Lehmann and M. O. Rabin. On the advantages of free choice: A symmetric and fully distributed solution to the dining philosophers problem. In *8th ACM Symposium on Principles of Programming Languages*, pages 133–138, 1981. DOI: 10.1145/567532.567547.

Two algorithms in which randomization is used to break symmetry are presented. The first algorithm, called the Free Philosophers Algorithm (page 57), satisfies deadlock-freedom while the second, called Courteous Philosophers Algorithm, satisfies starvation-freedom. 59

[35] M. C. Loui and H. Abu-Amara. Memory requirements for agreement among unreliable asynchronous processes. *Advances in Computing Research*, 4:163–183, 1987.

Among other results, it is proved that there is no consensus algorithm that can tolerate even a single crash failure in an asynchronous shared memory system in which only atomic read/write registers are used. See also [20]. 29, 85, 98

[36] A. McIver and C. Morgan. *Abstraction, Refinement and Proof for Probabilistic Systems*. Monographs in Computer Science, Springer, 2004. DOI: 10.1007/b138392.

An approach is presented for modeling and reasoning about computer systems that incorporates probability. 47

[37] G. E. Moore. Cramming more components onto integrated circuits. *Electronics*, 38(8):114–117, 1965. DOI: 10.1109/jproc.1998.658762.

In this article Gordon Moore predicted exponential growth in the density of transistors in integrated circuits. Since then, this prediction, known as the "Moore's Law," went on to become a self-fulfilling prophecy. 7

[38] M. Pease, R. Shostak, and L. Lamport. Reaching agreement in the presence of faults. *Journal of the ACM*, 27(2):228–234, 1980. DOI: 10.1145/322186.322188.

The first paper that defines the agreement problem (from Chapter 5). Among several results, it proved the lower bound result from Section 5.3, and provided a matching upper bound (see also [33]). 29, 38, 85, 99

[39] G. L. Peterson. Myths about the mutual exclusion problem. *Information Processing Letters*, 12(3):115–116, 1981. DOI: 10.1016/0020-0190(81)90106-x.

A simple two-process solution to the mutual exclusion problem is presented. The solution is also modified to solve the n process case. 17, 99

[40] S. A. Plotkin. Sticky bits and universality of consensus. In *Proc. 8th ACM Symposium on Principles of Distributed Computing*, pages 159–175, 1989. DOI: 10.1145/72981.72992.

Shows that sticky bits are universal: They can be used to transform sequential specifications of arbitrary objects into wait-free concurrent implementations. 85

[41] M. O. Rabin. The choice coordination problem. *Acta Informatica*, 17:121–134, 1982. DOI: 10.1007/bf00288965.

The choice coordination problem with k alternatives is introduced. The paper focuses mainly on the case of $k = 2$. 47

[42] M. O. Rabin. Probabilistic algorithms. In J. F. Traub, Ed., *Algorithms and Complexity: Recent Results and New Directions*, pages 21–39. Academic Press, New York, 1976.

Randomized algorithms were introduced, which had a tremendous impact on the design of algorithm in all areas of computer science. 59

[43] S. P. Rana and D. K. Banerji. An optimal distributed solution to the dining philosophers problem. *International Journal of Parallel Programming*, 15:327–335, 1986. DOI: 10.1007/bf01407879.

The LLR algorithm is introduced (page 55), and it is shown that this algorithm allows the maximum achievable concurrency. 59

[44] M. Raynal. *Algorithms for Mutual Exclusion*, MIT Press, 1986. Translation of: Algorithmique du parallélisme, 1984.

A collection of some early algorithms for mutual exclusion. 17

[45] M. Saks and F. Zaharoglou. Wait-free k-set agreement is impossible: The topology of public knowledge. *SIAM Journal on Computing*, 29, 2000. DOI: 10.1137/s0097539796307698.

Among other results, the authors prove the impossibility result for set-consensus as stated on page 29. See also [7, 28]. 29, 96, 99

[46] G. Taubenfeld. On the nonexistence of resilient consensus protocols. *Information Processing Letters*, 37(5):285–289, March 1991. DOI: 10.1016/0020-0190(91)90221-3.

In [20], it is proved that there is no consensus algorithm that can tolerate even a single crash failure in an asynchronous message-passing system. The paper presents a new, simple, and elegant proof of this important impossibility result. 29

[47] G. Taubenfeld. Computing in the presence of timing failures. In *Proc. of the 26th IEEE International Conference on Distributed Computing Systems (ICDCS)*, July 2006. DOI: 10.1109/icdcs.2006.21.

Timing failures refer to a situation where the timing constraints are not met. The author investigates the ability to recover automatically from transient timing failures, and presents time-resilient solutions to the mutual exclusion and consensus problems. See also [24, 25]. 30, 98

[48] G. Taubenfeld. *Synchronization Algorithms and Concurrent Programming*, Pearson/Prentice-Hall, 2006, 423 pages.

Dozens of algorithms for solving a wide variety of basic and advanced synchronization problems are presented, their correctness is formally proved and their performance is analyzed according to precise complexity measures. 17, 59, 71, 85

[49] G. Taubenfeld. Tight space bounds for ℓ-exclusion. *Distributed Computing*, 27(3):165–179, 2014. (Also in *LNCS 6950*, pages 110–124, DISC 2011). DOI: 10.1007/978-3-642-24100-0_8.

It is proven that to solve the ℓ-exclusion problem for $n \geq 2$ processors, $2n - 2$ bits are necessary and sufficient. The correct algorithm presented on page 91 is derived from an ℓ-exclusion algorithm which appears this paper. 93

[50] A. E. Treat. Experimental control of ear choice in the moth ear mite. In *Verh. XI. Internationaler Kongress für Entomologie*, pages 619–621, 1960.

Includes an example where the choice coordination problem from Section 6.1 occurs in nature. See page 42 for details. 47

Author's Biography

GADI TAUBENFELD

Gadi Taubenfeld is a professor and past dean of the School of Computer Science at the Interdisciplinary Center in Herzliya, Israel. He is an established authority in the area of concurrent and distributed computing and has published widely in leading journals and conferences. He authored the book *Synchronization Algorithms and Concurrent Programming*, published by Pearson Education. His primary research interests are in concurrent and distributed computing. Gadi was the head of the computer science division at Israel's Open University; member of technical staff at AT&T Bell Laboratories; consultant to AT&T Labs—Research; and a research scientist and lecturer at Yale University. Gadi served as the program committee chair of PODC 2013 and DISC 2008 and holds a Ph.D. in Computer Science from the Technion—Israel Institute of Technology.

Index

Printed in the United States
by Baker & Taylor Publisher Services